YOU'RE THE VOICE
40 MORE DAYS WITH GOD

REBECCA ST. JAMES

YOU'RE THE VOICE

40 MORE DAYS WITH GOD

REBECCA ST. JAMES

THOMAS NELSON PUBLISHERS

Nashville • Atlanta • London • Vancouver

Published in Nashville, Tennessee, by Thomas Nelson, Inc., Publishers, and distributed in Canada by Word Communications, Ltd., Richmond, British Columbia, and in the United Kingdom by Word (UK), Ltd., Milton Keynes, England.

Concert photos by: Scott Livermore and Stephen L. Roebuck

DEDICATION

This devotional book is dedicated to the church as a whole, for allowing us to serve you and partner with you in ministry; it is truly a joy. Continue to boldly let His voice be heard! I also want to dedicate this book to my parents, whose love and devotion to God, and to each other, daily inspire me.

CONTENTS ♛

ACKNOWLEDGMENTS

"Then (Jesus) said, 'Go into the world. Go everywhere and announce the Message of God's good news to one and all.'" | Mark 16:15 The Message |

Lord Jesus, thank You for life and the opportunity to love and be loved by You. Lord, we commit to You this book as we have from the beginning and ask that it will accomplish what You will it to in people's lives. May each word encourage every reader to imitate You, live a life of godly love, and be "the voice" that You call us to be.

I love You so much,
Your daughter,

Rebecca

THANKS TO:

First of all, thank You to the love of my life, my Lord Jesus, who to me is the reason for everything.

To my family, immediate and extended—life with you guys is a circus—but a wonderful one! Especially to Mum and Dad, the boys, Libby, and my cousin "Matty-Boy"! Thanks for the memories; I love you all greatly.

To Dale, who has been the most essential "comrade" in the writing of this book. You have been such an encouragement to us as a family, and we appreciate all your hard work. Thank you for your faithfulness to God and to us.

To my friends, church family, and "home-office" team for everything you are to the life of this ministry. A special thanks to Vic and Marg, who have seen us through so many challenges and joys. And to my best friends, Karleen and Kylie—you two mean so much to me. Also thanks to Zach for the unique part you played in the "People Talk" sections.

To Curtis, Rob, Cindy, and the Thomas Nelson bunch for all your support. We are so pleased to be aligned with you in this unique way of serving Jesus. Keep on!

To James Chesser for your genius—keep seeking the Truth.

And last but not least to Tedd T., Wes, Dan, Eddie, and all the folks at ForeFront and Ambassador, especially Wes, Dan, and Eddie. Thanks for your generosity to us. In a big way, you make so much of what we do possible. Stay the course.

And to you, the reader, and everyone who prayed with us for this devotional . . .

May God bless you and keep you,
May His face shine upon you
And give you peace.

Love in Christ,
Rebecca St. James
Isaiah 30:15

FOREWORD

I'm a big fan of Rebecca St. James, but not for the reasons you'd expect. Oh, I really like her music, even if I'm a forty-something parent of two teens. But what I appreciate about Rebecca is how she speaks to young people in a way that makes the Christian life cool and exciting.

That point was driven home to me when I took my children, Andrea, fourteen, and Patrick, thirteen, to see Rebecca in concert in Colorado Springs, Colorado. I have been following her career ever since she appeared on the cover of *Brio*, Focus on the Family's teen magazine for girls.

Midway through her concert, Rebecca, a twenty-year-old from Australia, asked the audience to sit down. "I'd like to tell you about this ring I'm wearing," she said, pointing to a gold band on the ring finger of her right hand.

"It's a Promise Ring, and when my parents gave it to me, they said it was to symbolize my commitment to wait until marriage to have sex. I can tell you right now, I will be waiting for that special person God has planned for me!"

I clapped and cheered like everyone else in the sold-out auditorium, and I was impressed that Rebecca would make such a bold stand. But if you see her in concert or spend some time with her (as I've been fortunate to do), you'll find out that her faith is not something she brings out for display when she's striding along a stage. Nope, she's living out her faith in Christ every day, and that's why Rebecca is qualified to write *You're the Voice: 40 More Days with God.*

You're going to like this book, and I know Andrea and Patrick will too!

—Mike Yorkey

Mike Yorkey is editor of *Focus on the Family* magazine and author of a cover story on Rebecca and her family in the July 1997 issue.

WHY 40 MORE DAYS?

It has been encouraging to receive letters, get E-mail, and talk with people at my concerts who have studied through my first book, *Forty Days with God*. Many people have asked why the book is 40 days, rather than 30 days, since it takes a month to make a habit of something. My answer is that 40 days refers to a period of testing—disciplining ourselves to develop the habit of staying in His Word, having a daily time with God. Some have commented, "The study was great. I've gone through all of it and have developed a daily quiet time habit. Now what? Are you going to write another book?"

Others have expressed thoughts similar to these: "I know you receive a lot of mail and can't write everyone back, but maybe you could respond to people's questions through a book." I really enjoy the intermission part of my concerts in which I get to field questions from the crowd, but I thought another book might be a good way to respond to more people. Thus, *You're the Voice: 40 More Days with God* was born.

Stand strong,
Rebecca St. James
Acts 20:24

P.S. You may notice in this book we've added a new section called "People Talk." In it are quotes mainly taken from letters people have sent me that I think we can all learn from and be encouraged by. If you would like to write to me and share what God is doing in your life, please send your letter to:

Rebecca St. James
P.O. Box 1741
Brentwood, TN 37024

or E-mail me at:

http://rsjames.com

Concert Bookings: Ambassador:

Telephone: (615) 370-4700

Internet: 76135.3421@compuserve.com

FIRST THINGS FIRST

Before we venture into the book, I'd really like to encourage you to pray this prayer of commitment with me . . .

Lord Jesus,

Thank You so much for loving me and dying for me—even when I don't deserve You at all.

Lord, I commit myself to You. Come into my life, change me, break me. Make me new. Make me whole. Please forgive my sin and purify my heart.

Jesus, I believe You died on the cross and rose again three days later and one day I will live with You forever.

Meanwhile, help me to stand for You, to shine for You, and to make a difference in Your strength. Help me not to be silent, but to be bold about You and to let Your truth be known.

Use me, God. Show me how to love and to serve You.

**I love You so much.
In Jesus' name,
Amen**

1 ABBA (FATHER)

REBECCA TALKS During Christmas a couple of years ago I was at my grandparents' house in Australia, and I saw a magnet of the Old Irish Blessing on their refrigerator. It begins, "May the road rise up to meet you . . ." It really inspired me, and later I wrote it in my diary. A few months after that, when I was back in the States and was really praying about the right lyrics for this song, I remembered the Irish prayer. It made me realize that's what God does for us—He makes the road rise up to meet us, He looks after us. The word *Abba* means "Daddy" in Aramaic, the language spoken in Jesus' day. The fact that we can call God our "Daddy" is a wonderful thing. This is especially true for friends I have known who have grown up without a father figure in their lives or a father who wasn't really a "dad" to them.

"I'm feeling like the eagle that rises . . ." The first verse of the song was inspired by a mural I have in my room. It has eagles flying across the sun. As I was sitting in my chair looking up at the mural, the words just came into my head. . . . One of the verses that's really given me strength for a number of years is Isaiah 40:31. I love the part at the end of that chapter that talks about God giving strength to the weary and increasing the power of the weak. People often ask me where I get my inspiration for my songs. "Abba (Father)" was inspired by a magnet, a mural, a verse, and above all, prayer.

LYRICS FROM "ABBA"

I'm feeling like the eagle that rises,
Flies above the earth and its troubles.
Oh yes he knows that there are valleys below
But under his wings there's a stronger power.
Oh Father—You are my strength,
On You I wait upon.

Chorus
You make the road rise up to meet me,
You make the sun shine warm upon my face.
The wind is at my back and the rain falls soft.
God I lift You high—You are my Abba.

Running in this race to the finish line,
The only road for me is the narrow.
Not gonna stop or even look to the side.

When I fix my eyes on You, Jesus.
Oh Father (Abba), You are my strength
Now more than ever.

Repeat Chorus

When you've run too far—(and the road is long),
Can't walk another mile—(He is waiting)
Hope in Him again—(He'll renew you).
Then you will rise, gather up your wings and fly.

Repeat Chorus

Do you not know?
Have you not heard?

He gives strength to the weary,
To those who hope in Him,
They will soar like eagles.

PEOPLE TALK I was really excited to get a letter from a girl in Canada who had used the song "Abba" to worship God. She shared:

> One evening here on my farm, the sun was again performing God's imagination while setting. In my room "Abba" was playing so I had that song in my head. I went and stood out on my back porch, which faces west, so I was able to see the sun set. An extremely light rain was falling and the wind was so soft. So, standing there in the rain and wind, I started to sing, "Abba," and God was so there with me.

One of the major goals of my music is to help lead others in worship. Praise God! I met a twenty-four-year-old dancer at the "Spring Celebration" at Paramount's Great America theme park in Santa Clara, California. She related the following story:

> I was at my dance studio all by myself, pacing the floor, looking for inspiration for a particular dance I had to choreograph. I just kept praying, asking God to help me with it because I know that He is faithful. I was reading in Romans 8 and came to the part that talks about "Abba." I got so excited when I saw that verse, because God is my Daddy. And it was as if He said, "I'm gonna provide this for you." I couldn't help but just cry, "Abba, Abba, Abba!" He's awesome. ✳

GOD TALKS "For you did not receive a spirit that makes you a slave again to fear, but you received the Spirit of sonship. And by him we cry, 'Abba, Father.' The Spirit himself testifies with our spirit that we are God's children. Now if we are children, then we are heirs—heirs of God and co-heirs with Christ, if indeed we share in his sufferings in order that we may also share in his glory." Romans 8:15—17 NIV

MORE TIME WITH GOD

 Isaiah 40:29–31;   1 John 1:10–13;
Galatians 4:1–7;   1 John 3:1–2

 YOU TALK TO GOD

• What does it mean to me that God is my "Daddy"?

• One time when He really provided strength and hope when I thought I could go no farther was . . .

• As an heir of God and coheir with Christ, I get to share the following:

  • Salvation
    Knowing that makes me feel . . .

  • Sufferings
    Knowing that makes me feel . . .

  • Glory
    Knowing that makes me feel . . .

• Abba, thank You for adopting me into Your family. As Your child, help me today in the following ways . . .

2 SELFISHNESS VS. SERVANTHOOD

REBECCA TALKS Once when I was in California, I was asked in the question and answer time of my concert, "What do you think of Kurt Cobain's suicide?" At first I didn't know what to say. I really prayed that God would give me the right words.

I basically answered that Kurt Cobain (lead singer/songwriter for the punk rock group "Nirvana," who shot himself in April 1994) was an example of someone who absolutely lived for self. His death was the ultimate end to his own selfishness. When we decide to live for ourselves rather than choosing to live God's way, that's exactly what we do—condemn ourselves to destruction. To some extent, selfishness always leads to death of some sort. If you allow selfishness to have its way, you are really letting yourself slowly die inside. God's way is life—not death.

The opposite of selfishness is servanthood. One biblical phrase that comes back to me a lot is: "poured out like a drink offering." That's really what Jesus did—He poured out His whole life for us. On those days when I feel weary, I often remind myself of that phrase. It's sometimes tough, but in God's strength and power, we can do it! We can battle selfishness by serving God and others. 𝕲𝕲𝕲

PEOPLE TALK Someone reminded me of the importance of unselfishness when she said, "Please, always keep a servant's heart. It's one of the first things Jesus asks for."

An attitude worth having every day comes from a song I learned as a child:

> Brother, let me be your servant,
> Let me be as Christ to you.
> Pray that I might have the grace
> To let you be my servant too.

I love the mind-set that Mother Teresa shows when she says, "I am not important."

GOD TALKS "But even if I am being poured out like a drink offering on the sacrifice and service coming from your faith, I am glad and rejoice with all of you."

Philippians 2:17 NIV

MORE TIME WITH GOD

 Numbers 15:1–10; John 12:1–3;
Philippians 2:1–8; 1 Timothy 4:6–8

 YOU TALK TO GOD

Lord, help me daily to pour out my life as a drink offering that is pleasing to You:

• A gift I bring to You in worship . . .

• A part of my selfishness I plan to give up to You . . .

• Someone I plan to serve this week . . .

• Some practical ways I plan to carry out my service plan are . . .

3 ARE YOU AN ENCOURAGER?

A youth pastor from Oregon actually proposed to his fiancée in the middle of one of my concerts. Afterward he asked me, "If you could talk about one thing that kids today need more than anything, what would that be?" The biggest thing I believe young people need today is hope and encouragement.

It's amazing how God uses other people to encourage us in the little things. For instance, last Christmas I flew back to Australia on my own for the first time. I was extremely scared about changing terminals in L.A. Right before I got off the plane, I prayed that God would protect me. As soon as I walked into the terminal and asked the attendant where to find Air New Zealand, a man came up directly behind me and asked how to get to the exact same place for the exact same flight. It ended up that he escorted me the whole way to the gate! God looks after His kids.

While on that trip to Australia, I wrote this in my journal,

REBECCA'S JOURNAL

Whenever I've heard stories lately about the things God has done in people's lives, I've been encouraged by them. I think that's why God stresses fellowship so much—because He knows we need encouragement through one another. Today I read a verse I'd never noticed before that summed all that up rather nicely— "that you and I may be mutually encouraged by each other's faith" (Rom. 1:12 NIV). ✱

PEOPLE TALK A teenage girl from Pennsylvania E-mailed with these words:

It was actually God who brought me to you. I found you on the Internet! I was looking at some other Christian musicians' web pages, and I "accidentally" clicked on a link to your page. But I don't think it was an accident. God knew what He was doing! As time went on, I bought your music, and fell in love with your ability to bring forth truth in a ministry. I have kept up with what you are doing and have written letters to you. Then one day I was very surprised to see a letter from you to me. You wrote to encourage me to keep up with a small ministry of mine that I had shared with you. Thanks for all the encouragement!

I don't remember who said this, but I think it's true: "God has called us to be cheerleaders, not competitors."

"Our only goal is to serve others to reach their goal."— Josh McDowell

"You must encourage one another each day. And you must keep on while there is still a time that can be called 'today.'" Hebrews 3:13 CEV

MORE TIME WITH GOD

 Acts 15:30–33; Ephesians 6:21–22;
1 Thessalonians 5:11–14

YOU TALK TO GOD

• One person God has really used to encourage me in my faith is . . .

• Some of the ways I've been encouraged by this person are . . .

• Someone I feel God has called me to encourage is . . .

• Some ways in which I can do that are . . .

• To encourage means to "build up," rather than to "tear down."

• I repent of the following ways in which I have torn others down . . .

Lord, help me this week to spend more time not competing, but building others up. I praise You for all that You do to encourage me!

4 THAT'S WHAT MATTERS

REBECCA TALKS While doing a Bible study called The Mind of Christ, I was challenged to evaluate my possessions—things I own or maybe would like to own. One of the things that first came to mind, that we own as a family, is our farmhouse. This is what I wrote in relation to a quote in the study that said, "God's desire is to move your possessions from ownership to stewardship":

I feel that we are basically doing that with our house–we have given it to God and opened it as a home to friends, family, and people we feel God has called us to have under our roof. The only things I can think of that I would be freaked out if I lost were:

1. My Bibles
2. My harmonica (because I would be "harmonicaless" for my first song in concert!)
3. My purse (because it would be such a pain to cancel and renew debit cards, etc.)
4. My journals (or this study book because it has writing in it from my heart)

Also, I would like a car eventually (but it's not a big deal if I don't get one).

LYRICS FROM "THAT'S WHAT MATTERS"

I read about this guy once,
He seemed to own the earth.
As far as big shots go and people in the know, well
He was definitely top of the list.
Anything he wanted, he'd get it,
Society's dream,
Had lots of stuff, had lots of money,
But you know what's funny? He said it all was useless.

Meaningless—meaningless,
He said, "Everything is meaningless . . .
A chase after the wind."

Chorus
Don't wish for a better day,
Be glad and use the one you're in.
Fear God and do exactly what He says,
That's what matters.
All else fades like the flowers.

Well, he'd tried pleasure,
There was nothing in that.
He built houses and gardens and parks,
What good did it do?
Just got him more depressed.
Meaningless—meaningless,
He said, "Everything is meaningless . . .
But this is what I learned in all my years.

Repeat Chorus

Meaningless—meaningless,
He said, "Everything is meaningless . . . .
A chase after the wind."

Don't wish for a better day,
Be glad and use the one you're in.
Fear God and do exactly what He says,
That's what matters.
All else fades away.

Meaningful—meaningful,
Life holds new meaning
When God becomes the center of it all.

I read about another man once,
He came to save the earth.
You know I got to meet Him, Jesus;
He revolutionized my whole entire life.

Repeat Chorus

PEOPLE TALK   I received an E-mail from someone last fall that said:

I totally agree with your song "That's What Matters." I had a bit of fame recently. It was great at first, but after a while I needed something bigger to happen. I began to feel depressed, until I prayed to God for help. He showed me that He is what matters, and that no material things or accomplishments will make me happy without God.

GOD TALKS   "Now all has been heard; here is the conclusion of the matter: Fear God and keep his commandments, for this is the whole duty of man."

Ecclesiastes 12:13 NIV

MORE TIME WITH GOD

 Proverbs 11:4,24–25,28; Ecclesiastes 2:1–11;
Luke 12:13–21; 1 Timothy 6:6–10

 YOU TALK TO GOD

• On a "love of money" scale of 1-10 (1 being money-carefree and 10 being money-hungry) where would I place myself?

1   2   3   4   5   6   7   8   9   10

• What is something I "just had to have" last year that I now think is "meaningless"?

• Lord, this is one thing I think You are trying to teach me regarding my possessions:

• Help me today to demonstrate my desire to put You first before anything that I own. It won't be easy, but I need You to help me . . .

5 FIVE ESSENTIALS FOR STANDING STRONG

REBECCA TALKS The most important time for us in each concert is the commitment time at the end of the evening. People are really encouraged to get serious with God and give everything to Him. Every time I see someone come forward to make a decision, I stand in awe of God. I know that it is the Holy Spirit's work, and nothing that I have done. I can talk and share as much as I want, but it's only God who can draw people to Himself.

I lead those who have come to make a decision in a time of prayer. Then I share 5 essential things that have encouraged me to stand in my faith. They are:

1. **DIG INTO THE BIBLE**

It really is our "instruction book for life." The deeper we dig into it, the more we know how God wants us to live. I encourage you to start out by reading a chapter a day and really absorb the Word of God. That Book rocks!

2. **DIG INTO PRAYER**

What a privilege to actually be able to talk with the Creator of the world! Pour your heart out to Him. Give Him your burdens and everything that's going on in your life. He's God–He can handle it! Prayer is so powerful!

3. **STICK CLOSE TO CHRISTIAN FRIENDS**

We all need Christian friends to hold us accountable. We can't stand alone. I'd encourage you to be a part of, or start, a small accountability group or Bible study. Stick close to people who will not let you stand still in your walk with God.

4. **GET RID OF JUNK IN YOUR LIFE**

If there are certain things you are watching, listening to, or reading that God does not want you to have in your life, get rid of them. If you don't, those things are going to hurt your relationship with God. We've got to remember that once we get something in our minds, we can't get it back out.

5. **GET INVOLVED IN CHURCH**

It's so important that we are grounded in a Bible-based Christian church where we can grow spiritually and give out the light and love that we have in Jesus. We all need to be a part of a church that loves God, loves one another, and loves the lost. This world desperately needs Him!

I received a very encouraging letter from a girl in North Wales, Pennsylvania, recently. She wrote about her desire to see her good friend come to Jesus. She said:

> I wanted to save (my friend) but I finally realized that was not my place. Only God could do that. For a few years I have been praying about it. When you came in concert, she came with me. On the hour-and-a-half drive there, we were talking about the fact that nothing in life seems to be free. My mom said that Jesus is free. . . . At your concert that night, (my friend) shot out of her seat when you gave the altar call. When she came back to her seat she was so broken. I said, "See, the best thing of all is free!" It reminded me so much of James 4:7–12—she became broken before God, and He lifted her up! (My friend) has a lot of adjusting to do, but it's one day at a time, one step at a time. I can pray and keep her accountable. It's not going to be easy for her, but if she stays with Jesus it will be worth it!

GOD TALKS "With all this going for us, my dear, dear friends, stand your ground. And don't hold back. Throw yourselves into the work of the Master, confident that nothing you do for him is a waste of time or effort." 1 Corinthians 15:58 The Message

MORE TIME WITH GOD

 Psalm 105:1–4; Proverbs 27:17; Matthew 4:4;
Acts 2:41–47; Ephesians 4:29–5:7

 YOU TALK TO GOD

- Of the 5 essentials Rebecca mentions, the weakest area in my own life is . . .

- I will plan to improve in that area by taking the following steps today:

- One of the instructions in God's Book that I need to obey is . . .

- In order to communicate more with my heavenly Father, I commit to do the following each day:

- A couple of Christian friends who can help keep me accountable are:

- Some junk in my life that I must throw away includes:

- A ministry I plan to pursue in my church is . . .

6 A Great Team

Someone asked me recently in concert, "Why do you bring your family on the road with you?" I love being part of a big family and having them all on the road with me. It's so encouraging to know that I'm just a part of a big team that serves God together. Road life can get pretty draining if you don't have people around who can help you stay grounded and accountable. There's something about having six younger siblings that really helps you in the "grounded" department!

In 1 Corinthians 12, Paul talks about the body of Christ. In our family, we all have our own part to play. My dad is my manager, which is great, because I don't have to worry about the business side of what I do. He also road manages each of our tours and helps with the sound. Mum is one of my biggest accountability partners and keeps everyone in line. Daniel, my 18-year-old brother, programs and runs the computer-driven light show and sings backup vocals on a couple of songs. Ben, fifteen, also helps with lights and is our resident photographer and "video guy." Then, there's Joel, thirteen, who is our stage manager and backup singer on several songs, Luke, ten, operates a spotlight and aids our drummer, and five-year-old Libby just, loves everybody, plays, and looks cute. Finally, there's my seven-year-old brother, Josh, who sets up the Compassion International booth and quotes in one of the songs, "Until you find something worth dying for, you're not really living." ⑥⑥⑥

PEOPLE TALK

A friend from Oklahoma observed:

> I was able to watch your crew (or should I say family) as you prepared for the concert in our church. Suddenly it dawned on me that this wasn't just Rebecca's concert, it was everyone's concert. . . . All of you worked as a great team! I watched everyone work together. Thanks for making your concert more of a ministry that involved everyone!

GOD TALKS

"Be even-tempered, content with second place, quick to forgive an offense. Forgive as quickly and completely as the Master forgave you. And regardless of what else you put on, wear love. It's your basic, all-purpose garment. Never be without it.

"Let the peace of Christ keep you in tune with each other, in step with each other. None of this going off and doing your own thing. And cultivate thankfulness."

Colossians 3:13–15 The Message

MORE TIME WITH GOD

Romans 12:10, 16; 15:5–7;
Ephesians 4:15–16; 1 Peter 3:8

YOU TALK TO GOD

- When it comes to being a team player, I'd say that I'm
  - ☐ the quarterback.
  - ☐ in the trenches.
  - ☐ dropping back for the punt.
  - ☐ a player-coach.
  - ☐ not even on the playing field.
  - ☐ in preseason training.
  - ☐ other _____ .

- Concerning unity with others, the thing I do best is . . .

- One of the things I have learned about myself by working with others is . . .

- The thing I need to work on most in this area is . . .

7 RESTING BEFORE GOD

REBECCA TALKS Sometimes I get concerned when it comes time to write songs for a new album. Songwriting can be a rather challenging experience! Recently I've been thinking and praying about songs for an upcoming record. One day I wrote in my journal:

REBECCA'S JOURNAL

Something really cool just happened. After praying on my knees next to my bed, I felt prompted to read Mum's *Life Application Bible* on the subject of waiting on God. I looked up one of the first entries, Psalm 40:1–4. Verse 3 says, "He put a new song in my mouth, a hymn of praise to our God. / Many will see and fear and put their trust in the LORD" (NIV).

That was the verse that stood out to me. I felt it was a real encouragement from God and a promise. When there is something that is out of my hands, I simply have to trust God for His inspiration and timing. It's like getting out on the edge. When I'm seeking a message God wants me to communicate to others in my ministry, I can't force it or make it happen. I felt God through this verse saying that He was going to put a new song in my mouth and that through His work, many would see and fear and trust Him. I want to go on experiencing God.

PEOPLE TALK A friend's dad (also a former Sunday school teacher of mine) wrote to encourage me to rest before God. He shared Isaiah 30:15 with me in the letter, and that passage has since become a real "theme" verse for me. He also told me about a Christian retreat he had attended where the whole time they fellowshipped, ate together, enjoyed God's creation—but in silence. He said it was one of the most powerful experiences of his life.

At one of my concerts, a guy shared:

Someone at church told me that he thought God wants me to rest in the promises He has for me. Through various things in my life He's teaching me to rest. I'm realizing that I don't have it all worked out down here. That's kind of hard to learn because I've always been a worrywart. God is showing me to learn to relax and let Him take care of everything.

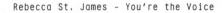

GOD TALKS

"This is what the Sovereign LORD, the Holy One of Israel, says:

'In repentance and rest is your salvation,

in quietness and trust is your strength,

but you would have none of it.' . . .

Yet the LORD longs to be gracious to you;

he rises to show you compassion.

For the LORD is a God of justice.

Blessed are all who wait for him!" Isaiah 30:15, 18 NIV

MORE TIME WITH GOD

 Genesis 2:2–3; Psalms 4:4–5; 46:10;

Lamentations 3:25–26; Matthew 11:28–30; Hebrew 4:4, 9–11

YOU TALK TO GOD

• The best vacation I ever had was . . .

• The last time I really was still before God was . . .

• Something He taught me at that "rest stop" was . . .

• One thing that really makes me anxious and causes me to not put my trust in God is . . .

• Lord, help me to give that "rest stealer" to You this week by . . .

8 HEAD BETWEEN OUR KNEES?

REBECCA TALKS I was really challenged one day while reading 1 Kings 18. Elijah had just confronted 850 false prophets by saying, "How long will you waver between two opinions? If the *Lord* is God, follow him; but if Baal is God, follow him" (v. 21 NIV). God showed that He was the true God by making fire fall from heaven when Elijah prayed for it to happen. An awful drought had just about ended. And Elijah said to Ahab, "Go, eat and drink, for there is the sound of a heavy rain" (basically, celebrate!). So Ahab went off to feed himself, but Elijah stayed behind. He "climbed to the top of (Mt.) Carmel, bent down to the ground and put his face between his knees" (vv. 41–42 NIV).

What total humility in the face of triumph! Most of us would have gone off to celebrate a great victory, but Elijah humbly sought God instead. What an example to us of real humility and brokenness before God! 666

PEOPLE TALK One of the most frequently asked questions in my concerts is: "What do you do to stay grounded and humble when you're up on the stage and in the spotlight?"

Really, prayer is a big key for me—praying before everything and knowing that I can't do it on my own. Another thing that helps me a whole lot is keeping daily in the Bible, reading verses like, "Don't push your way to the front; don't sweet-talk your way to the top. Put yourself aside, and help others get ahead" (Phil. 2:3 The Message) or "Get down on your knees before the Master; it's the only way you'll get on your feet" (James 4:10 The Message).

"Don't believe your own publicity." I love that challenging quote. We can't afford to take ourselves too seriously—we must know that "this all surpassing power is from God and not from us" (2 Cor. 4:7 NIV). ✕◊✕

GOD TALKS "And Elijah said to Ahab, 'Go, eat and drink, for there is the sound of a heavy rain.'" So Ahab went off to eat and drink, but Elijah climbed to the top of Carmel, bent down to the ground and put his face between his knees." 1 Kings 18:41–42 NIV.

MORE TIME WITH GOD

 Proverbs 16:3, 5; Luke 14:1–11;
John 3:26–30; 2 Corinthians 3:17–18

 YOU TALK TO GOD

- When I think of a role model in my own life who is humble, I think of . . .

- Something I have been told by others that I do well is . . .

- One way to keep that talent in perspective and give God the glory is . . .

- What happens when I don't give God the glory?

Lord God, strip away my pride. Teach me to receive others' praise humbly and deflect all the glory to You.

9 YOU THEN ME

I believe that one of the biggest challenges in life is overcoming selfishness. Our generation has been sold the lie that in order to live a happy life, all we have to do is think about "me" and "how I feel," when the opposite is the truth. I think that's why Jesus stressed so often the importance of serving others. Real joy comes from forgetting ourselves.

When I first sat down with Tedd (my producer), to talk about the *God* album, he asked, "What do you sense God is calling you to say through your ministry?" One thing that continued to come through as a topic was selflessness—putting others first. Whenever we would look through potential lyrics for the album, we would put it through this litmus test and ask, "OK, does this line up with the things we really feel God wants us to say on this record?" When we came across the song "You Then Me," immediately it was a great fit. It was kind of a neat and different way to say that we really need to put others first.

LYRICS FROM "YOU THEN ME"

It's my turn, it's not your turn,
It's my turn, get outta my way,
It's my turn, go on complain,
I'm comin' through anyway.
Don't ask me why I'm like this
But lately I'm wonderin' if
It'll come to pass
That the last shall be first and the first shall be last.
Then the voice says . . .

Chorus
Here's the way it oughta be,
You then me then you then me.
Well, I pray one day we'll all agree
And take it you then me, then you then me.
Life could go you then me, then you then me.
It's easy, you wait then go,
It's easy, so make your move,
It's easy, don't clown around,
You could've gone six times by now.
But no sir, you gotta be a pain
Or is this your way of sayin'
We should all cool down
And be more like the man who was born back in

Bethlehem town?
I betcha He'd say . . .

Repeat Chorus

If we could only put You first
Maybe this ugly trend could one day be reversed.

It's your turn, it's not my turn,
It's your turn—well let's just say
We'll trade off—first you, then me
Then after that, we might agree.
Let's try it, it could be good,
And what if one day it should
Really come to pass
That the last shall be first and the first shall be last?
Betcha we'd say . . .

Repeat Chorus

In a very honest letter, someone expressed these thoughts:

(I used to be) extremely self-centered. I didn't do really bad things, but I cared only about me. I thought happiness came from making myself feel good. I was wrong. Christ came into my life and He showed me that it is lifting others up that really counts.

"The fruit of prayer is a deepening of faith, and the fruit of faith is love, and the fruit of love is service, and the fruit of service is peace . . . works of love are works of peace."— Mother Teresa of Calcutta

GOD TALKS "He sat down and summoned the Twelve. 'So you want first place? Then take the last place. Be the servant of all.'" Mark 9:35 The Message

MORE TIME WITH GOD

Proverbs 25:6–7,27, Matthew 18:1–5;
Mark 10:35–45; 1 Peter 5:5–6

YOU TALK TO GOD

• The area of my life in which I tend to be the most competitive is . . .

• Someone I have hurt by putting myself first is . . .

     • To reconcile with him or her, I need to . . . .

     • I plan to do the following . . .

     by_____ .
        date

• Dear God, help me this week to follow the example of Jesus in putting others first. One thing I will do today to lift someone else up is . . .

10 WASHED BY THE WORD

REBECCA TALKS   Ten minutes ago I was out in the garden planting some pota-toes with some friends. Now I have to tell you, when you plant potatoes, you get rather messy! My hands were absolutely covered with packed-on dirt! Praise God for water and soap! This relates to an analogy I want to share with you. One day while I was reading Ephesians 5, it really struck me that if we are not in the Bible, we are not cleansed. The Bible convicts us, challenges us, and shows us where we are dirty. It shows us where we need to clean up our lives. When we don't get into the Word daily, we are continually getting filthy. What a challenge to "wash up"!

James 1:5 says, "If any of you lacks wisdom, he should ask God, who gives gen-erously to all without finding fault, and it will be given to him" (NIV). When we read God's instruction book, we receive wisdom. We can pray this prayer in faith:

> Grant me wisdom, Lord,
> Wisdom to know Your will,
> Wisdom to know what You want,
> Wisdom to know what You are saying.

PEOPLE TALK   A nineteen-year-old from Louisville, Kentucky, wrote with some very honest thoughts when she said,

> Sometimes it's very hard for me to feel worthy of His love. I don't really believe that He can use me. I know that Jesus is just looking for people that are willing, but I just feel like I couldn't do anything for Him. (Sometimes) I read my Bible and pray and I still don't seem to be getting any closer to God. . . . It's very upsetting to me 'cause I love God with all my heart and I want to be used by Him so much. I just can't seem to get past this problem. Do you have any advice?

I can relate . . . sometimes when I read my Bible, it does not exactly feel as if much is sinking in; but the truth is that it is sinking in. The Bible says that God's Word will not return void (Isa. 55:11). And if I've learned anything about Bible reading, it's that it comes down to disciplining ourselves to digging daily into God's truth—and God will honor His promise. We will see the long-term effects of it in our lives.

MORE TIME WITH GOD

Ephesians 6:17; Titus 3:3–7; Hebrews 4:12–13; 10:19–22; James 1:5–7; Revelation 22:12–14

 YOU TALK TO GOD

• Some parts of my life that are impure, in need of God's washing, are:

   • In my thought life . . .

   • In my words . . .

   • In my actions . . .

• I remember a time when I had no clue in a certain situation, and God provided wisdom. This is what He did:

• In order to take a "spiritual bath" daily I commit to do the following:

Lord, I look forward to the time when I will live with You in heaven forever, in a place where nothing impure exists. Help me to remember that forever begins today as I seek to be cleansed by Your Word.

11 Do You Need to Be Broken?

I've been really challenged by the Promise Keepers men's movement. From what I've seen, the men that have been impacted by this "awakening" are fair-dinkumly (Australian for "seriously") on fire for God. I really believe that one of the big reasons for the revival in these men's lives is that they are being challenged to get on their faces and be broken before God. It's like the verse in 2 Chronicles 7:14, where God promises, "If my people, who are called by my name, will humble themselves and pray and seek my face and turn from their wicked ways, then will I hear from heaven and will forgive their sin and will heal their land" (NIV).

That means responding to others out of humility and not out of pride. That means listening to others' opinions and treating them as better than our own. God really wants to mold all of us—male, female, young, and old—into what He created us to be. We all need to be broken before God. Dwight L. Moody once said, "God can do great things with broken pieces, provided He gets all the pieces." We can't hold anything back. We must lay it all down, broken as it may be, at His feet.

PEOPLE TALK I recently received a letter from a man in Rochester, Indiana. He shared how God worked through a difficult situation to break him and cause him to depend on his heavenly Father:

> After graduation I entered the Marine Corps to become a fighter pilot. I thought I was pretty cool. I was tall, fit, and girls seemed to think I was attractive. . . . Sad to say, it was easy to lose track of God and just as easy to lead a less than virtuous life. I'd probably be living that way now, but on July 23, 1994, God spoke to me loud and clear. I was flying a fighter trainer with a friend on what was supposed to be a routine flight. As we were taking off, the jet caught fire and we were forced to eject about twenty feet above the ground. My parachute opened just before impact, and although I survived, I fractured my spine. I landed near the wreckage of the jet and had to crawl away from the flames. My friend wasn't as lucky. He died when his parachute didn't open and he collided with a grove of trees. . . .

I spent the next two years in therapy, both physical and psychological, trying to heal from the accident. . . . I had to claw my way out of depression, but thankfully, I discovered God. He's real and He saved me. . . . I still carry a lot of pain, but God is always there when I need Him. God is Good!

In his letter, this man went on to share a poem he had composed at the Ichthus Festival in Kentucky this past spring:

FOREVER BEGINS TODAY

I sat in my room, praying last night, "God, will You speak to me?"
I read my Bible, went to church yesterday, but still I'm a little afraid.
Please help me, God, I'm sinking fast; sin's easy in this world.
I've stumbled, I've fallen so many times, abused body and flesh, Your temple.
I've lied to friends, my family, stained my soul, and even more.
Will this be my last plea when I die, "Will I meet Your Son?"

"My child, I sent Him to die for you, He bled, a spear pierced His side.
To hell and back He carried your sins, and even then, we knew you."
Yes, we knew you at the dawn of time, your heart never far from our sight.
By your faith, salvation secure, your soul bathed in heavenly light.
Took pain to help you see the Father and Son you were missing.
The Holy Spirit showed the way to a cross that before was just history.
And never forget we'll give you the strength
To feel heaven here on earth; forever begins today."

© Carl D. Hogsett Jr. Used by permission.

GOD TALKS

"The sacrifices of God are a broken spirit;
a broken and contrite heart,
O God, you will not despise." Psalm 51:17 NIV

MORE TIME WITH GOD

 Psalms 34:17–20; 61:1–3;147:3,6;
Isaiah 66:2

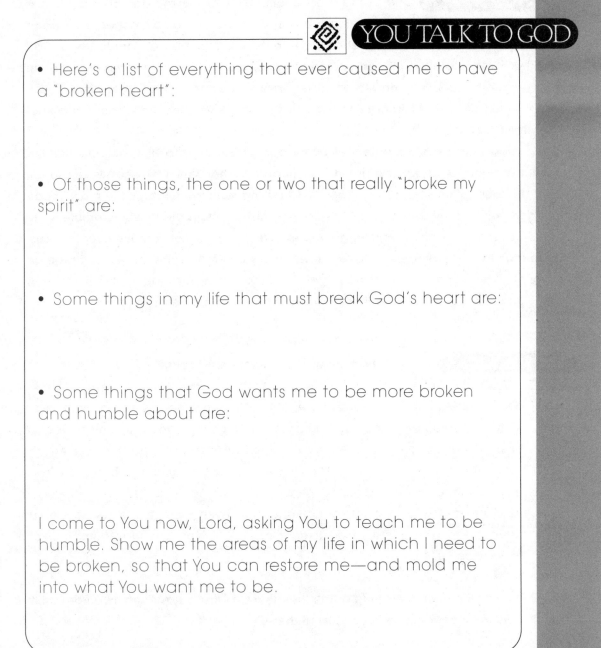

YOU TALK TO GOD

• Here's a list of everything that ever caused me to have a "broken heart":

• Of those things, the one or two that really "broke my spirit" are:

• Some things in my life that must break God's heart are:

• Some things that God wants me to be more broken and humble about are:

I come to You now, Lord, asking You to teach me to be humble. Show me the areas of my life in which I need to be broken, so that You can restore me—and mold me into what You want me to be.

12 GET SERIOUS

REBECCA TALKS One of the most challenging things my dad says is, "Unless you're going forward in your relationship with God, you're going backward." A good way to give ourselves a spiritual checkup is to ask, "Am I more passionate about God now than ever before?" In the last couple of years, as I've been able to travel, I've been encouraged by seeing teenagers who are really serious about God. They have a genuine love for Him, and it's impacting the way they live—what they talk about and what they stand for.

God calls us all to surrender every part of our lives to Him, holding nothing back. No matter what age we are, it is so important that we know what we stand for, what the foundation of our lives really is. Choosing to follow Christ is the most important decision you will ever make. The sold-out Christian life is the most incredible, wonderful adventure. I want to challenge you to give every part of your life over to Jesus. There may be things you need to lay down at Jesus' feet. Maybe there's compromise in your life, and God is calling you to get rid of those things. Whatever it is, life is short and God is calling us to make these decisions now and not delay.

PEOPLE TALK   A guy from Texas E-mailed me and said,

On October 31, 1996, a car disrupted the path of my friend's car, thus running him off the road and causing his death. A friend to many, only one noticeable thing was missing in his life—Jesus. I cannot bear to think that I let a friend die without the love of God in his life. (Since that day) my goal has been to minister God's wonderful love not just to friends, but to strangers as well. Your enthusiastic and straightforward insights encouraged me even more to get out there and preach the Word—and to do it right now! . . . Even one day could make a difference. ✳

I heard another interesting quote the other day that says, "Even if you are on the right track, you'll get run over if you just sit there."

GOD TALKS "I can't impress this on you too strongly. God is looking over your shoulder. Christ himself is the Judge, with the final say on everyone, living and dead. He is about to break into the open with his rule, so proclaim the Message with intensity; keep on your watch. Challenge, warn, and urge your people. Don't ever quit. Just keep it simple.

"You're going to find that there will be times when people will have no stomach for solid teaching, but will fill up on spiritual junk food—catchy opinions that tickle their fancy. They'll turn their backs on truth and chase mirages. But you—keep your eye on what you're doing; accept the hard times along with the good; keep the Message alive; do a thorough job as God's servant." 2 Timothy 4:1-5 The Message

MORE TIME WITH GOD

 Romans 12:11; 2 Corinthians 6:1–2; Revelation 3:15–16

YOU TALK TO GOD

• Am I more passionate about God now than ever before? What proof do I have of my growth in Jesus this past year?

• If I were to compare my spiritual growth to a car on a road, I'd say that I'm . . .

- ☐ on the right track.
- ☐ driving in reverse.
- ☐ pulling in for a tune-up.
- ☐ on a fast track to nowhere.
- ☐ carrying excess baggage in the trunk.
- ☐ cruising at a safe speed.
- ☐ other _____ .

• What things do I need to get rid of to get back on the right track?

• What is God telling me to do now and not wait?

13 FEEDING YOUR MIND

REBECCA TALKS I love to read. In my bag that travels with me everywhere I always have two Bibles (two different translations), my diary, and usually a Christian book of some sort. I especially love Christian historical fiction because I believe we can learn a lot from the past. We are so fortunate to be able to read and to fill our minds with things that are going to grow us in our relationship with God and help us in our lives. Our minds are really like the most incredible computer you can imagine! They remember everything. We need to be so careful that we're filling our heads with things that are pure. We need to be set apart for God to be used by Him.

It may be that sometimes we just need to say to God, "Lord, purify my mind. Help me to start over today and resist the temptation to fill my mind with things that are not of You. Give me a distaste for evil, and more and more of a love and desire for You." I love the prayer that says, "Create in me a pure heart, O God, and renew a steadfast spirit within me" (Ps. 51:10 NIV).

PEOPLE TALK Billy Graham was once asked, what he would do differently if he had the chance to live life over again. His simple answer was that he would watch less television.

A man from Pakistan wrote because he had seen an article about our family in *Decision* magazine, which is distributed by the Billy Graham Evangelistic Organization. He said:

> Thank you for your magazine. It is a great gift of God for me and my family. We are blessed by reading it. We are also sharing it with our friends and the Word of God is working in a strange way in our lives.

GOD TALKS "Don't waste your energy striving for perishable food like that. Work for the food that sticks with you, food that nourishes your lasting life, food the Son of Man provides. He and what he does are guaranteed by God the Father to last. . . .

"In the same way that the fully alive Father sent me here and I live because of him, so the one who makes a meal of me lives because of me. This is the Bread from heaven. Your ancestors ate bread, and later died. Whoever eats this Bread will live always." John 6:27, 57–58 The Message

MORE TIME WITH GOD

 Proverbs 15:14–15; Jeremiah 31:33–34; Matthew 7:17–20

Ephesians 4:22-24; Colossians 3:1–2

YOU TALK TO GOD

• If I were to compare my spiritual growth to eating, I'd say that I . . .

☐ try to survive on one meal a week.

☐ eat two to three meals a day.

☐ have fasted so long I should not be alive.

☐ exist on junk food.

☐ am trying to live on bread and water.

☐ am eating more regularly.

☐ other _____ .

• To really feed my mind on things that honor God, what do I need to do less of?

• Junk that I allow in my mind often crowds out the "meat and potatoes" of God's Word. What junk food is clogging my spiritual brain cells?

• Besides the Bible, what else should I be feeding my mind?

• Lord God, with Your help, I plan to do the following . . .

14 MY PURITY RING

REBECCA TALKS A few years ago my dad presented me a purity ring, a neat reminder of the commitment I've made to wait until marriage to have sex. I wear it on the ring finger of my right hand. It also lets others know of the commitment I've made to wait. The safest way to maintain purity is to decide, prior to temptation, to remain pure.

My cousin Matt, who is also my age, saw my ring and heard me talk about it. He decided he wanted a physical reminder of his commitment too. So I got to present him with a purity chain, and we had a special ceremony with speeches and all! It was so cool.

I want to encourage you to keep waiting for the person God has for you. That is absolutely God's way. He designed us, and He knows what's best for us. If God says it, I believe it.

PEOPLE TALK Because I have spoken publicly about my virginity, I have received some very sad letters from girls who didn't give their virginity away, but had it taken from them through rape. I know that God's heart breaks for those who have been hurt in this way. Our Father does not want His children to live in guilt for something they did not do!

Others have written to me and asked things like, "Where do you draw the line concerning technical virginity (how far is too far)?" Well, I challenge guys and girls to think of the other person as someone's future husband or wife, and then ask questions such as, "Should I be behaving this way with someone else's future spouse?" We have to think of the future.

A guy from Alberta, Canada, wrote with these encouraging words:

It's good to know that there are people out there who are virgins. It is very reassuring to know that it's all right to wait. Some of my friends outside the youth group have at times put pressure on me to have sex. I'm proud to say that I haven't given in. You help give strength and hope that I can wait until I meet that special someone I want to marry.

GOD TALKS "God wants you to be holy, so don't be immoral in matters of sex. Respect and honor your wife. Don't be a slave of your desires or live like people who don't know God. You must not cheat any of the Lord's followers in matters of sex. Remember, we warned you that he punishes everyone who does such things. God didn't choose you to be filthy, but to be pure. So if you don't obey these rules, you are not really disobeying us. You are disobeying God, who gives you his Holy Spirit."

1 Thessalonians 4:3–8 CEV

MORE TIME WITH GOD

 Psalm 119:9-10; Ephesians 5:30–5;
Titus 1:15–2:6; Hebrews 13:4

 YOU TALK TO GOD

• Father, I pray for the strength to maintain sexual purity in a world of filth.

  • Help me in the things I watch:

  • Help me in the things I think:

  • Help me in the things I say:

  • Help me in the things I do:

• Father, I also pray for the purity of my future mate . . .

Thank You for Your perfect example of purity. I want to be like You.

15 CAUGHT IN THE MIDDLE

I meet so many people whose lives have been impacted by divorce. This past year it's become even more of a reality to me as I've gotten to know my keyboard player, Chris C., whose parents divorced when he was 16. I asked him how he coped with it and what he would share with you on this subject. This is what he said:

> I never thought it would happen to me. When I was younger, I felt real hurt that my parents would divorce. It was a time to really search my heart and ask, "Where do I go from here?" The song, "Caught in the Middle" came out of what I was going through at the time, but I didn't think the song would ever be heard by anyone else. Then I realized that there are so many others who have gone through the same situation and need to know that they're not alone.

For those of you who have either been divorced or are children of divorce, I want to encourage you by saying that you don't have to live in that hurt. You can make something out of your life. You can't do anything to control what has happened to you, but you can control how you respond to it. I know firsthand that to release your anger and forgive your parents is not an easy thing to do. But, with God's help, you can do it!

LYRICS FROM "CAUGHT IN THE MIDDLE"

Mommy's over here and Daddy's over there,
Caught in the middle you wonder if they understand.
To them it's no big deal but still there's a part of you they steal;
By letting go they're tearing you apart.

Chorus
Caught in the middle of a love that's torn apart,
Standing there with just a broken heart.
Can we make the good times stay
Or have they really gone away?
A happy ending seems so far away.

Echoes of the voices that once were there
From the joy and laughter that we used to share.
If it's not within their sight have they gone without a fight?
Has the love that was there simply left for good?

Repeat Chorus

Words by Chris C. and Thomas M. Rose. © 1992 by Christopher E. Comtois and Thomas M. Rose. Used by permission.

All the time, Chris talks with people who have been touched by his song. It is so important for them to realize that when they're "caught in the middle," it is not their fault. All too often they allow the feelings of blame to turn inward so that they may even feel ugly and worthless. If you or someone you know is in this situation, please know that Jesus feels your pain. He wants to help. He wants to dry up the tears and give you hope to carry on.

★

GOD TALKS "The Lamb in the center of the throne will be their shepherd. He will lead them to streams of live-giving water, and God will wipe all tears from their eyes." Revelation 7:17 CEV

MORE TIME WITH GOD

 Psalms 10:12–14, 17–18, 68:5–6;

2 Corinthians 1:3–7;   Colossians 3:13

 YOU TALK TO GOD

• Some of the hurts that I need to let go of are . . .

• A person I need to forgive is . . .

• Someone I know who has been impacted by divorce is . . .

• I can encourage this person in these practical ways:

• Lord, I come to You now, praising You for being my perfect Father. Thank You for providing comfort in the past through these tough situations:

16 THE POWER OF PRAYER

In our Western civilization, the attitude in life is very much "go, go, go." It's hard to discipline ourselves to take daily time out with God. But it's so very, very important. While we are on the road, before each concert we have devotions as a team. We pray, sing a worship song, and read from *My Utmost for His Highest* (a devotional book by Oswald Chambers). We also have prayer huddles right before we go onstage!

It is essential for me to sit down every day, whether on a plane, in a car, in a hotel room, or really anywhere, and just talk to God and ask Him what He wants to say to me. I know that if I do not fill up with Him, then I have nothing to give. I always pray before doing interviews, even with those who are from the secular media. They are often very surprised that I would ask to pray, but I know that I can't do the interview without giving it to God first.

I have seen total miracles happen through prayer. For instance, we especially prayed for the right people to be in the band for the "All About God" tour. And, in really different, unique ways, God confirmed the perfect people to be involved. First of all, Brad, originally from Oregon, plays guitar and is the band leader. He also happens to be a youth pastor. Pretty cool. Then there is Virginia native Andrew, our phenomenal drummer, who has a heart for God and can really rock! Christopher C. from Melbourne, Florida, has traveled for a number of years ministering in schools. He plays keyboards on the tour and also performs some of his own songs. And Tracy, our bass guitarist, could really be a pastor in a church because he has so much wisdom! I have grown spiritually through knowing these guys and to me they are a real tribute to the power of prayer.

PEOPLE TALK I received a very encouraging letter from a girl who lives on the island of Aruba. She shared the following:

I (have been) a Christian since I was 7 years old. I love to read the Bible. My favorite books are Psalms, Romans, and Esther. I love to talk the Word to others so they can know the Lord also. My father and my mother are also Christian, but my sister is not. I pray that she could find the way of truth someday. My grandfather always prays for his children to come to (know the Lord). Some have come, but there are still others who are in the world—but they will come, I am sure of that. . . . mi ta wak bo despues (see you later). ★

A girl wrote to me about a friend of hers who had asked why Christians thank God when He makes a bad day a good one. I answered:

I know for me personally there have been quite a few times when I've been down about something or have a bad attitude and I've prayed that God will change my heart, and within ten minutes it happened. There was nothing that physically cheered me up—it was all because of prayer. ◎

GOD TALKS "Never stop praying, especially for others. Always pray by the power of the Spirit. Stay alert and keep praying for God's people. Pray that I will be given the message to speak and that I may fearlessly explain the mystery about the good news. I was sent to do this work, and that's the reason I am in jail. So pray that I will be brave and will speak as I should." Ephesians 6:18–20 CEV

MORE TIME WITH GOD

 Proverbs 15:8, 29;   Zechariah 4:6;   Acts 4:23-31;
1 Corinthians 2:1–5;   James 5:13–18

YOU TALK TO GOD

• When I think back over the past year, one thing about which I can say, "The only way it could have happened was because of God," would be . . .

• What is one time when I tried to do something for God and failed because I attempted it on my own strength and not His?

• Some things I really need to turn over to God in prayer are:

• Lord, I come to You today praising You for . . .

• I ask You to reveal Your power this week in the following situation:

17 HOLY FEAR

This is what I wrote in my journal recently on the topic of "fearing God":

REBECCA'S JOURNAL

I've felt kind of lacking in that true "fear" department. I think it's so easy (I know for me anyway) to get into a "buddy-buddy" relationship with God and not give Him all the respect and honor that He's due. Well, I think part of the problem I've had with having a holy fear of God is that I don't fear anything much in life. I feel very secure in my family and in my relationship with God.

But lately, I've figured out one particular thing that I fear. It came to me that maybe part of fearing God is not coming into His presence with total confidence, but spending time realizing who God is, and who I am. In essence, One is absolutely, unfathomably huge and the other as insignificant as an ant in comparison. 🌀🌀

That day, I read Isaiah 8:13, 17 in my Bible. What a great challenge to truly fear God. I've read that one definition of *fear* in the dictionary is "profound reverence and awe, especially toward God."

PEOPLE TALK "We are in bondage to what we fear." I heard someone say this once and I think it is so true. But really, being in bondage to God, in submission to Him, is the most free place we can be in life.

King Jehoshaphat of Judah said, "Now let the fear of the LORD be upon you. . . . You must serve faithfully and wholeheartedly in the fear of the LORD." 2 Chronicles. 19:7, 9 NIV

GOD TALKS "The LORD Almighty is the one you are to regard as holy,
he is the one you are to fear,
he is the one you are to dread. . . .
I will wait for the LORD,
Who is hiding his face from the house of Jacob.
I will put my trust in him." Isaiah 8:13, 17 NIV

MORE TIME WITH GOD

 Psalm 34:7–11; Proverbs 19:23; Malachi 4:1–2;
Luke 12:4–7; Hebrews 12:28–29; 1 Peter 1:17

 YOU TALK TO GOD

• As a child, some of the things I feared were (check all that apply):

☐ Monsters
☐ Thunder and lightning
☐ The "bogeyman"
☐ The doctor or dentist
☐ Snakes
☐ The dark
☐ The devil
☐ Spiders
☐ My dad
☐ Ghosts
☐ Fire
☐ Big dogs
☐ Other _____

• Why does my generation not fear God as we should?

• The attributes about God that cause me to bow down in awe and holy fear of Him are . . .

• As I focus on Your holiness, I thank You today for . . .

Lord God, help me not to take You for granted, but to come to You with a holy respect for who You are and what You do. Teach me to revere Your name.

18 INNER BEAUTY

REBECCA TALKS When I first came to the States, one of the biggest things that shocked me was how image-conscious people were, how concerned they were with being dressed up. In Australia, you can go to the mall and see people in scruffy T-shirts, no makeup, and no shoes. Here, you go to the mall, and it's show time! Lately, I've been feeling a real desire just to be beautiful to God—to focus more on inward, rather than outward, beauty. Sometimes you see people who are beautiful on the outside, and you look in their eyes and see that they are empty. God wants us to become beautiful on the inside like His Son.

In my journal one day I wrote,

REBECCA'S JOURNAL

Lord Jesus, I love You so much. You are beautiful. Lord, make me beautiful inside, as You are—no hidden motives, no sin messing up the light, hiding it; no compromise, just pure love for You. Show me more how to adore You, how to worship You in my daily living. Make me more convicted of You and the needs of others. I love and adore You.

PEOPLE TALK I received a letter not too long ago from a 13-year-old girl who represents so many others out there. She said,

My older sister is really pretty. I wish that I was pretty. My mom said that I look like something the dog drug in. She's telling the truth. Why did God make me so ugly? You're pretty and so are all my friends. It's not fair.

I think every female knows other girls who are more beautiful, more outgoing, or generally more attractive. I'm sure guys can relate to the same male insecurities. The challenge for us as Christians is to focus on what is important—being beautiful and pleasing in God's eyes. Man looks at the outer appearance, but God looks at the heart.

GOD TALKS "What matters is not your outer appearance—the styling of your hair, the jewelry you wear, the cut of your clothes—but your inner disposition.
Cultivate inner beauty, the gentle, gracious kind that God delights in. The holy women of old were beautiful before God that way." 1 Peter 3:3-5 The Message

MORE TIME WITH GOD

 Proverbs 31:30–3; Isaiah 53:1–3; Matthew 23:25–28;
Ephesians 3:14–19; 1 Timothy 2:9–10

 YOU TALK TO GOD

• What are some things I do to draw attention to myself?

• Things I wear . . .

• Ways I alter my appearance . . .

• Why am I so concerned with what others think about how I look?

• What does God think about me?

• Some parts of my inner life that need to be beautified by God are:

Help me, Father, to follow the example of Your Son, who didn't spend time attracting others by His appearance, but by the beauty that was within Him.

19 THOSE WHO HAVE GONE BEFORE

Here's something I wrote in my journal last December:

REBECCA'S JOURNAL

Today I was reading out of Chronicles (I've been challenged to read more from the Old Testament). At first when I looked at the books of Chronicles, I thought, *What am I going to learn from this?* Basically, the books are about genealogies (family trees). But on the way to the studio today I was reading my Bible—and was so encouraged to think that all these people are my spiritual forefathers! Really I just have to be faithful to continue on in that heritage of people following after God. It made me excited and challenged in my duty. But what a joy that duty is—to follow God and leave our lives and cares to Him! Then, out of the blue, I turned to Psalm 90, (v. 1) which says, "Lord, you have been our dwelling place throughout all generations." (v. 1 NIV) Pretty amazing.

All of us have adults in our lives who have encouraged us, prayed for us, and helped us "live the life." We need to treat them with respect and thank God for the godly example they have been to us. Our generation so desperately needs role models worth following.

PEOPLE TALK A 76-year-old grandmother from Lone Star, Texas, wrote to me with these words:

> I have been reading your devotional book and am so grateful to God for you and your witness and dedication. I'm a grandmother with 8 grandsons and 2 great-grandsons—not a little lady in the bunch! May God richly bless your every endeavor.

Wow! I am humbled that a grandmother would be reading my book! It really should be the other way around. There is so much wisdom we can learn from those who have walked the road and gone before us.

A guy who has really supported our ministry wrote to me and shared this in regard to his family legacy:

The other night at my church, my pastor showed my dad and me a quote he had written down from my grandpa, who died a couple of years ago at the age of 95. He was a pillar of faith just waiting to meet his precious Jesus. My grandpa's words of wisdom are as follows: "One thing I think we fall short in thanking God for is tribulation. I think we have someone dependable to come to." It means so much to me to have that heritage of faith.

GOD TALKS

"These are things we learned from our ancestors,

and we will tell them to the next generation.

We won't keep secret the glorious deeds

and the mighty miracles of the LORD.

God gave his Law to Jacob's descendants,

the people of Israel.

And he told our ancestors to teach their children,

so that each new generation would know his Law

and tell it to the next." Psalm 78:3-6 CEV

Rebecca St. James - You're the Voice

MORE TIME WITH GOD

 Job 8:8–10;   Psalms 71:17–18;   145:3–7;
2 Timothy 1:5;   3:14–15

 YOU TALK TO GOD

• Something I own that has been "handed down" from my ancestors is . . .

• Who are some mentors in my life whom I have learned from?

• What are some of the ways I have benefited from their words, prayers, and actions?

• What specific people in my life can I set a godly example for?

Thank You, Lord, for the godly examples You have given me to follow. Help me to please You today as I follow in their footsteps.

20 ENJOYING GOD

REBECCA TALKS I love God so much. He is truly the One that my whole life revolves around. That's why it's so important to me to worship Him daily, enjoy Him, grow closer to Him, so I don't lose that desire for Him. I think it's really interesting that the word *enthusiasm* (enjoyment) comes from two Greek words, *En theos*, which really means "in God." He is the reason for our enthusiasm. And, when we are enthusiastic, we are contagious!

One of my biggest delights in life is to take walks outside or even sit on the floor of my bedroom or hotel room and just talk to God as my best friend. Recently I was upstairs in our house getting ready to slow down for the night. I remembered I'd left something outside in the car. Grudgingly, I decided to go out and get it. As I walked out the door, I looked around and witnessed the most incredible, peaceful, beautiful night—and up above shining down was a perfectly round full moon! It was as if God were saying, "Rebecca, stop. Take some time just to worship and be in awe of Me!" Those moments, whether it's splashing around in the creek, running through a field, or throwing up my hands in the air and reaching out to Him, are some of the most happy, joyful times of my life!

PEOPLE TALK An old Russian Proverb says, "He who has this disease called Jesus will never be cured."

In his book *You Gotta Keep Dancin'*, Tim Hansel has said, "Pain is inevitable, but misery is optional. We cannot avoid pain, but we can avoid joy."[1]

We must choose joy, even when it is difficult. Joy is so much deeper than happiness. It is not based on "happenings" but on the confidence we have that in God everything is going to be all right. And we can rejoice in that!

GOD TALKS "When the righteous see God in action
they'll laugh, they'll sing,
  they'll laugh and sing for joy.
Sing hymns to God;
all heaven, sing out;
  clear the way for the coming of Cloud-Rider.
Enjoy *God*,
  cheer when you see him!" | Psalm 68:3-4 The Message |

MORE TIME WITH GOD

 Psalm 37:4–6; 97:10–12; Habakkuk 3:17–19;
Zephaniah 3:14–17;   Philippians 4:4

YOU TALK TO GOD

• One of the most joyful people I know is_____ because . . .

• The last time I wanted to stand up and applaud God was when . . .

• Three things that God has done that really make me smile are . . .

    1.
    2.
    3.

• A few things in my life that tend to steal my joy are . . .

• If others were evaluating the joy in my life on a scale of 1-10, they would probably give me a _____ .

Help me today, Lord, to enjoy all the good things You have brought into my life. Teach me to delight in You even when things in my life are less than joyful.

21 WE CAN'T BE SILENT

REBECCA TALKS Last year a girl came up to me after a concert with tears in her eyes. She gripped my hand and said, "Rebecca, our generation is dying." Basically she was asking herself, "What am I doing about it?"

We can't afford to be silent about our faith any longer. We've got to be bold. We've got to let people know the truth about Jesus before it's too late. We are His voice. That's the message of the song, "You're the Voice," on the *God* album.

We really prayed for the video of that song to be powerful. This is what I wrote in my journal the night after filming the video:

REBECCA'S JOURNAL

Today was really a great day. God moved as we asked Him to. I felt prompted to tell certain people about the video, like my producer and (others in his) office, our youth minister at church and his team. I asked them to pray for us today. I had a few concerns, venturing into uncharted waters. God heard. As I said to Dad, it couldn't have gone better. God really allowed the director and me to be totally on the same page. It was really a "God day" and I'm extremely happy. Praise God for what He's done!

PEOPLE TALK

I received a lyric from a guy from Minnesota that I found convicting. I'd like to share it with you:

I was walking down the road today, I saw a friend I hadn't seen in a while.
He said, "Hey, how are you doing?"
I just said "Fine," and then he said, "What's new?"
I didn't tell him, I didn't tell him . . . about You.
I sat down for dinner at a local cafe. I bowed my head to pray.
A man up at the jukebox said, "Give me a break! What are you trying to prove?"

I didn't tell him, I didn't tell him about You.
My friend calls me once a year, I got a letter instead;
it was from his mother telling me that he was dead.
I didn't know quite what to do. All I did was cry;
'Cause I didn't tell him about the Lord before he died.

© 1988 by Tyler J. Lebens. Used by permission.

GOD TALKS "Be brave and strong! Don't be afraid of the nations on the other side of the Jordan. The LORD your God will always be at your side, and he will never abandon you. . . . The LORD will lead you into the land. He will always be with you and help you, so don't ever be afraid of your enemies." Deuteronomy 31:6, 8 CEV

MORE TIME WITH GOD

 Psalm 56:3–4;   Daniel 3:16–18;
Acts 1:8, 4:12–13, 18–20, 29

 YOU TALK TO GOD

• Some excuses I have used for not sharing Jesus with others include . . .

• If any of my family or friends died without being given the opportunity to accept God's grace I would feel . . .

• Five of my friends or family members who need to know Jesus are:

     1.

     2.

     3.

     4.

     5.

• Some practical ways I can share Jesus' love with them are . . .

• Father, forgive me for not talking about Your great love to others. Help me overcome my fear today as I reach out in the following ways:

Continue to remind me that You will go before me.

REBECCA TALKS While traveling so much these last couple of years, one of the things I've seen is that so many young people in my generation are looking for love in the wrong places. That's why I feel a big burden to encourage parents and teens, and at the same time myself, to work hard on our family relationships. I really believe that if my generation truly worked on finding love and acceptance in the home and in a relationship with God, they wouldn't be looking elsewhere for it.

I know one thing that has really encouraged me a lot as a teen is that we are very open and honest in our family—we talk about everything. I've found that there's real freedom in that kind of total vulnerability. Take Mum, for instance, who is one of my best friends. If I'm going through something, and I just don't know what to do, I'll find her folding laundry or reading or whatever she's doing and talk with her about it. Sometimes she'll have advice or a story from her life that relates to my situation, but sometimes she'll just listen or give a hug or a smile. That's encouragement—the built-in accountability factor God calls the family. 👁️👁️

PEOPLE TALK This past spring I had the opportunity to meet someone who had accepted Jesus at one of my concerts the year before. She stayed until 1:30 A.M. after our concert at Knott's Berry Farm in California so we could talk and pray together. What an encouragement that was! She shared about how much she had grown in the Lord in the past year and that one of the first things she did after giving her life to God was to reconcile with her family (after being estranged from them for a couple of years). In a letter to me she wrote:

> It's been a little over a month since I asked Him to come with me on my "jouney." It's been very challenging, but very cool. The challenging parts have been finding good, solid Christian friends to talk with. It hurts my heart so much to see people who claim they love Him and live for Him . . . then they put Him in the closet when certain people come around . . . God is telling me to be content with the (Christian friends) I have for now.

Growing up I always seemed to have a younger sibling in my arms. The *big* baby here is Joel (now 13) and Ben is standing beside me.

My seven-year-old brother, Josh, quoting from the song "Carry Me High" . . . "Until you find something worth dying for, you're not really living."

My producer, Tedd, and me in the studio where we recorded the *God* album.

Bibles in hand, preparing to go onstage at a festival. Joel doing his part as our stage manager, my best friend, Kylie, ready to pray with me, and Josh preparing to do his part too.

One of the joys of my life . . . worshiping God with thousands of other teenagers.

Singing and sharing at a Fourth of July event outside of Dallas.

The whole family standing in front of the van at our Aussie home.

My family with my grandparents at the 1995 Dove Awards.

I was the flower girl at my aunt and uncle's wedding when I was four years old. I love this photo of my grandpa, brother Daniel, Dad, me, and Grandma.

Just a "little bitty girl."
Me at age one.

I *loved* dressing up
as a kid!

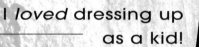

I respect my
great-grandmother so
much. (I dedicated my
first book, *Forty Days
With God*, to her
because of her love
and commitment to
Jesus.) This is a photo
of my great-grandma
and me at a Christmas
get-together.

One of the highlights of the concert is the question and answer time, where the audience can ask me anything they want. Let me tell you . . . it's always a surprise!

God . . . a passionate subject to sing about.

On the phone finishing up the devotional!

Since playing the guitar on "A Cold Heart Turns" on the *God* album (which was a miracle in itself!), I've enjoyed "Trying my hand at it" every now and then.

A concert shot taken with the band on the "All About God" tour.

A "quick pic" after seeing the hot springs
at Yellowstone National Park on a day off.
The entourage includes: my family
and me, some friends, "the Phelpses,"
from Australia, Kylie, the band and crew.

Getting ready to say
good-bye . . . Mum,
Dad, Nanna, Pop,
and me at
the Nashville
airport, ready to
go with all our
boxes of
merchandise
and gear.

A thoughtful moment with the band . . . "Fear God and do exactly what He says, that's what matters . . . all else fades like the flowers."

Working in the studio is a whole lot of work, but a whole lot of fun too!

The band and me in our "prayer huddle" before going onstage.

GOD TALKS "Each one of us needs to look after the good of the people around us, asking ourselves, 'How can I help?'

"That's exactly what Jesus did. He didn't make it easy for himself by avoiding people's troubles, but waded right in and helped out. . . .

"So reach out and welcome one another to God's glory. Jesus did it; now you do it!"

Romans 15:2–3, 7 The Message

MORE TIME WITH GOD

 Proverbs 19:20;   Malachi 3:16;
Ephesians 4:2–3;   Colossians 1:28

 **YOU TALK TO GOD**

• The people in my life whose acceptance of me means the most are . . .

• Something spoken to me by a Christian family member or friend that I really needed to hear was . . .

• One of the hardest things I've ever had to tell a Christian friend was . . .

• What are some practical things I can do to "look after the good" of those around me?

REBECCA TALKS In my early high school years, I had the chance to go on a mission trip with my youth group. We went to Chicago and held backyard Bible clubs, visited nursing homes and mental hospitals. That week really opened my eyes to the number of lonely and hurting people there are in this world. It made me realize that often all it takes is a smile, a handshake, or a kind word to make someone's day.

That experience also challenged me to think about the fact that we are truly "on a mission" whether we are formally on a mission trip or not. People are looking to us to be examples of Jesus' love, to be missionaries right in the here and now.

PEOPLE TALK I'm always encouraged to hear about some of the creative and unique ministries that people are involved in. Here are just a few I've learned of recently:

A 16-year-old girl from New Mexico said,

> My father, sister, and I are musicians. We are not all that great, but hey, we are not doing it for man, we're doing it for the Lord, right? My father plays the guitar and bass. My sister plays guitar, bass, and drums. I play drums and bass. I'm still learning, but I give it my all.

A guy from Vancouver, Washington, wrote,

> Last January I started chatting in the Rebecca St. James chatroom on your home page. Since then I've met some very wonderful people. Many people also come in there every day that need our prayers. There is a giant mission field on the Internet. Your chatroom is being used by God to witness to people. . . . God has begun a good work in me and I know that He is faithful and just to complete it. I know that he wants to use me to minister to people in need. . . . Please pray for me.

An eighth-grade guy from Bedford, Indiana, shared his ministry in these words:

> I started a Bible study in my school called Reality 101. It meets every Tuesday morning from 7:30 to 8:10 A.M. We have been averaging about 22 kids. . . . I have seen that Christian music is one of our more powerful tools. I also have a Christian radio program in the works! Keep up the good work.

GOD TALKS "After this, I heard the LORD ask, 'Is there anyone I can send? Will someone go for us?'

'I'll go,' I answered. 'Send me!'" | Isaiah 6:8 CEV |

MORE TIME WITH GOD

 1 Corinthians 12:4–7; 2 Corinthians 3:5–6;
James 2:14–17

 **YOU TALK TO GOD**

- What are five goals I hope to accomplish this year?

- How many of these are centered on God and serving others? How many are centered on me?

- I may have never thought of myself as a "minister" before, but now I realize that I am. What are some ministries God has called me to?

- Here I am, Lord. I want to go where You want me to go. Help me today to . . .

24 GOD'S WAY WORKS

REBECCA TALKS A few years ago, a friend of mine went off to college. I lost contact with her, and the next time I saw her was much later—outside a Kroger food store. Even before she said anything, I knew things weren't well. She had lost the sparkle in her eyes; something was different. That day I found out that she was pregnant, and it seemed that the father of the child and she were not going to marry.

Later on, after the baby was born, we talked on the phone about it. She told me that although she didn't regret her baby, she now knew why the Bible so strongly emphasizes living God's way, rather than following our own desires. I asked her that day if I could share her story with other people because we can learn so much from others' experiences. She really wanted me to share it and asked me to encourage people not to make the same decision she did. If my experience with my friend taught me anything, it's that God's way works—why mess with any other?

PEOPLE TALK I want to share another quote from *A Voice in the Wind*. Part of the reason I enjoy Christian fiction so much is that I get to see into godly characters' lives, their prayers, and how they relate to God. It really challenges me.

Hadassah had been captured by the Romans when they took over Jerusalem. In this particular scene, Marcus, the oldest son of the family she now served, was trying to challenge her to stop believing in God. He said to her, "Give up this faith you have in an unseen God. He isn't there."

Hadassah answered by pointing out the evidence of God and His perfect ways that are seen all around us. She responded,

"Can you see air you breathe? Can you see the force that moves the tides or changes the seasons or sends the birds to a winter haven?" Her eyes welled. "Can Rome with all its knowledge be so foolish? Oh, Marcus, you can't carve God in stone. You can't limit him to a temple. You can't imprison him on a mountaintop. Heaven is his throne; earth his footstool. Everything you see is his. Empires will rise and empires will fall. Only God prevails." [1]

GOD TALKS "Many are the plans in a man's heart, but it is the LORD's purpose that prevails." Proverbs 19:21 NIV

MORE TIME WITH GOD

 Psalm 111; Proverbs 14:12;   Isaiah 55:8–9;
Hosea 14:9; Acts 5:29–39

 YOU TALK TO GOD

• One time when God did something that has shown me "His way works" was . . .

• When I think about God's nature, a few of the things I see that just blow me away are . . .

• Father, I confess to You that I tried to go my own way when . . .

Lord God, I want Your thoughts to be my thoughts, and Your ways my ways. Help me as I strive to fulfill Your purpose for me.

25 UNEQUALLY YOKED?

REBECCA TALKS I remember, a few years back in youth group, playing (or watching) a particular game. One person would stand on a chair, while another stood on the floor at the feet of the first person. The person on the chair would try to pull the person on the floor up onto the chair. Unless the "floor person" was being extremely helpful, making it easy for him to be pulled up, then it was pretty much impossible. (Unless, I s'pose, the person on the chair was the muscle man of the youth group!) Then, the "floor person" would try to pull the "chair person" off the chair and usually succeeded within 10 seconds.

Our youth pastor would then use that physical illustration to show that often it's easier to be pulled down by the people we hang out with than to be pulled up or encouraged by them.

When you think about it, in a way, we are yoked to our friends. When bulls are yoked (bonded together by wood), if one decides to pull another way from the rest of the team, it just doesn't work. The same goes for us. If we are "bound" to friends that are going the wrong way, as much as we don't want to go, we're still going to be driven down the wrong path. We need to be so careful concerning whom we spend the bulk of our time with because, whether we like to admit it or not, our friends majorly affect how we live our lives. As my dad says, "We are who we hang with."

PEOPLE TALK Someone wrote a letter to me and shared,

Your message tonight is just what I needed. Because of it, I let go of a relationship with a non-Christian that had been controlling my life for a very long time.

Another girl shared her convictions this way:

If you date a non-Christian, you tend to get pulled away from your faith. If you date a Christian, you can help each other grow stronger in your faith. The temptation to date a non-Christian is strong, but I think you need to develop relationships with them first, so that they become Christians too.

MORE TIME WITH GOD

Galatians 5:7–9; 13-16;   Ephesians 5:5–11;
1 Peter 2:11–12, 17

YOU TALK TO GOD

• What evidence is there that the people I spend most of my time with draw me closer to God?

• What evidence is there that these people draw me away from God?

• What are some of the distractions to my spiritual life presented by those whom I date?

• Father, I want my body to be a holy temple, fit for service in Your kingdom. Help me to clean up this dwelling place for Your Spirit by doing the following:

Help me, Lord, to examine my dating relationships based on the standards found in Your Word.

26 FORGIVE AND FORGET

In a particular Bible study I've been doing recently, one of the most challenging topics has been forgiving hurts and grudges. I never really thought that I had any major hurts in my life. But thinking back, there was one particular thing that when I thought about it, there was a knot in the middle of my stomach. This is what I wrote in my diary in regard to this experience:

REBECCA'S JOURNAL

Just a second ago I was praying and thinking, *Lord, how do I forgive this person?* My first human reaction was to try and rationalize it—to make excuses for the person—but I knew in my heart that wasn't the way that would please God. He then reminded me of a verse He had shown me earlier today that said, "Forgive men when they sin against you, (and) your heavenly Father will also forgive you" (Matt. 6:14 NIV). It made me realize how much God had forgiven me, and if God has forgiven me for so many things, I can forgive this person for the small hurtful thing that was done to me! I feel such a sense of release. I can now think of that situation and there's no sad feeling in my heart. Freedom. Thank You, God!

PEOPLE TALK A 13-year-old guy from Syracuse, New York, shared this challenging poem with me:

My life points to the cross in more ways than one.
It's the direction that I'm headed, it's where I deserve to be.
But I see a shadow of a man hanging from that tree.
He's taken my place, He's where I deserve to be.
His blood flows down onto the ground.
His blood flows over me, makes me clean.
I don't deserve this, but it's the only way.
The shadow's gone,
He's lifted now, up to His eternal home.
I take a glance down on my hands,
Bloodstained,
I am clean,
Not dirty,
Not deserving.

I don't know who said it, but I believe it: "God's desire is to move your hurts from producing resentment to producing love."

MORE TIME WITH GOD

 Matthew 5:43–45; 18:21-35, Luke 17:3–4; Ephesians 4:31–32;   Colossians 3:12–13

 YOU TALK TO GOD

- Lord, I come to You now with my hurts. I pray for these people:

  for hurting me in the following ways:

  Help me to forgive.

- I desire to get rid of this resentment or bitterness in my life by . . .

- Now I ask You to help those whom I have hurt:

in the following ways:

Give me the courage to ask those I've hurt for forgiveness.

Help them to forgive.

27 COMPASSION

REBECCA TALKS Growing up outside Sydney, Australia, I have vivid childhood memories of visiting the city. The harbor bridge, the funny-looking white opera house, the people, and huge buildings. It was all very "Wow" to me. I enjoy thinking about times as a kid when I used to run around backstage with my brothers at concerts Dad promoted in those Sydney auditoriums.

But some of the experiences I remember the most are walks downtown with my family, seeing people begging for money. I felt so sorry for them, especially the ones who were in wheelchairs or were disabled. I remember thinking that it would be so cool if someday I could buy a house in Sydney where poor people could come, have a bath, put on clean, nice clothes, and have a place to stay. I thought (this sounds pretty cute now, looking back) I'd charge them 20 cents, because that's all they could afford!

I don't know whether God will lead me in the future to do something like that, or lead me to run an orphanage like I've always dreamed of—it's all in His hands. But to me, it's so important that I be faithful wherever God has put me, to show His love and compassion to everyone—young, old, rich, or poor—everyone!

PEOPLE TALK In Western civilization it's hard for us to imagine the kinds of needs there are in other countries when we have so much at our fingertips. Check out these statistics:

- 35,000 children die every day in the world from illnesses brought on by malnutrition. Ninety percent of these would have been preventable if the children just had clean water and sanitation.
- Every night 1 in 5 children around the world will go to bed hungry.
- One-third of the world's population are children under the age of 15.
- Eighty-five percent of those who come to Christ are under the age of 18.

A girl from Ft. Walton Beach, Florida, wrote and said, "So many times I've seen the Compassion or World Vision commercials and I feel so helpless 'cause there's no way I'd be able to support a child. (I'm only 12 years old!)"

But, you know, one way young people can help make a difference is by sponsoring children together. For instance, with Compassion, if you and 2 other friends were to sponsor a child together, it would only cost each of you about $8.00 a month.[1] There are so many ways in which we can show God's love and compassion to others—things like helping out in the community, mowing a neighbor's lawn for free, doing the dishes at home, or going on a mission trip. God really calls us to be Jesus with skin on. We've got to realize that we could be the only Jesus that some people will ever see.

GOD TALKS "This is how we've come to understand and experience love: Christ sacrificed his life for us. This is why we ought to live sacrificially for our fellow believers, and not just be out for ourselves. If you see some brother or sister in need and have the means to do something about it but turn a cold shoulder and do nothing, what happens to God's love? It disappears. And you made it disappear.

My dear children, let's not just talk about love; let's practice real love."

1 John 3:16–18 The Message

MORE TIME WITH GOD

Deuteronomy 15:7–11; Psalm 112:4–9;
Zechariah 7:8–10; Matthew 14:13–14

YOU TALK TO GOD

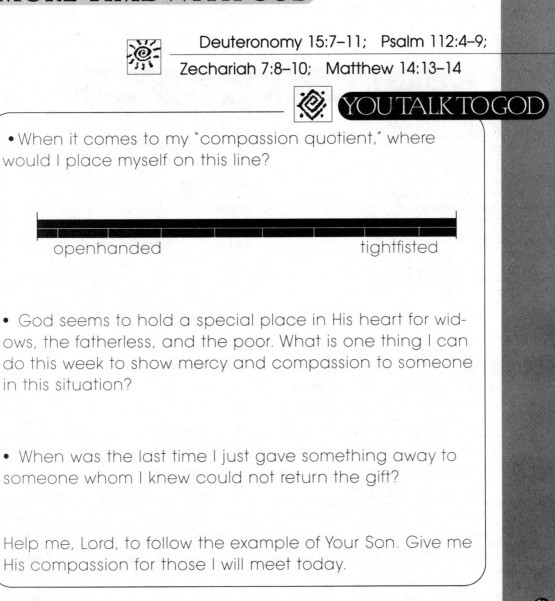

• When it comes to my "compassion quotient," where would I place myself on this line?

openhanded   tightfisted

• God seems to hold a special place in His heart for widows, the fatherless, and the poor. What is one thing I can do this week to show mercy and compassion to someone in this situation?

• When was the last time I just gave something away to someone whom I knew could not return the gift?

Help me, Lord, to follow the example of Your Son. Give me His compassion for those I will meet today.

28 A COLD HEART TURNS

REBECCA TALKS How many times do we look out the window on a sunny day and not stop to praise God for it? How many times do we see "minimiracles" or answers to prayer and not thank Him? I really believe so many times God "calls out" to us through everyday things and through His creation, and yet we don't hear because we're too busy or distracted. David said in Psalm 19:1, "The heavens declare the glory of God; the skies proclaim the work of his hands" (NIV). On this train of thought, the song, "A Cold Heart Turns" was inspired.

LYRICS FROM "A COLD HEART TURNS"

Power thunder, lightning bolts,
Rushing wind, a waterfall,
Baby's cry, a mother's tears,
Humming river, rustling leaves.

Chorus
He's calling loud and clearly,
He's saying, "Won't you hear Me?"
We see Him everywhere
And still we roll on by.

Winter snow, a fire's warmth,
A summer's day, a cold heart turns.
Peaceful place, a helping hand,
A kindly word, a smiling face.

Repeat Chorus

He was God but one of us,
A King who had a servant's heart,
Born to die so we might live.
His reason was His Father's will.

Repeat Chorus

Power thunder, lightning bolts,
Rushing wind, a waterfall,
Winter snow, a fire's warmth,
A summer's day, a cold heart turns.

Words by Rebecca St. James © 1996 Up In The Mix Music (a division of the ForeFront Communications Group, Inc.). (BMI)/Bibbitsong Music (administered By ICG). (BMI). All rights reserved. International copyright secured.

PEOPLE TALK The story about this song is a real miracle. My producer, Tedd T., shares the experience in his own words:

The creation of this song was one of the most amazing tangible ways in which we saw God work on the *God* album. We were about three-quarters of the way through with the record. One night Bec went into the front of the studio to work on some lyrics while I was getting some guitar tracks ready. She was just beginning to play guitar at the time. After about an hour, she came back and said, "Hey. I've got this idea I wanna run by ya." She was really excited about it. She said, "I think it's pretty cool. You ought to check this out. I'm not sure if it's all together yet. The lyrics need some work, and the melody's not quite there, but take a listen."

So she played this guitar part and sang the song basically as you hear it on the record. I just sat there; my jaw dropped and I said, "Becca, we've got to go back in the studio right now and record this." We stopped what we were doing and set up 2 mikes, one on the guitar and one on her vocal—and hit the record button. She played it straight down, having no idea what she was playing on guitar. She played all the guitars on that song and it was recorded in probably 7 or 8 minutes. I think we took a couple of passes and it was over . . . that blew me away. It was like, this is an amazing thing. We simply added a little keyboard part with it.

It was incredible to me that as we continued to put the whole process in God's hands, things like that would happen. That was one of the most amazing miracles in the recording of the *God* album. She was given this great arrangement, this great lyric, this great melody. Literally, the track that you hear on the record is no different from what we recorded that night.

GOD TALKS "Drop everything and listen, listen as he speaks: 'Don't turn a deaf ear.'" Psalm 95:8 The Message

MORE TIME WITH GOD

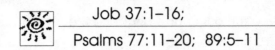

Job 37:1–16;

Psalms 77:11–20; 89:5–11

YOU TALK TO GOD

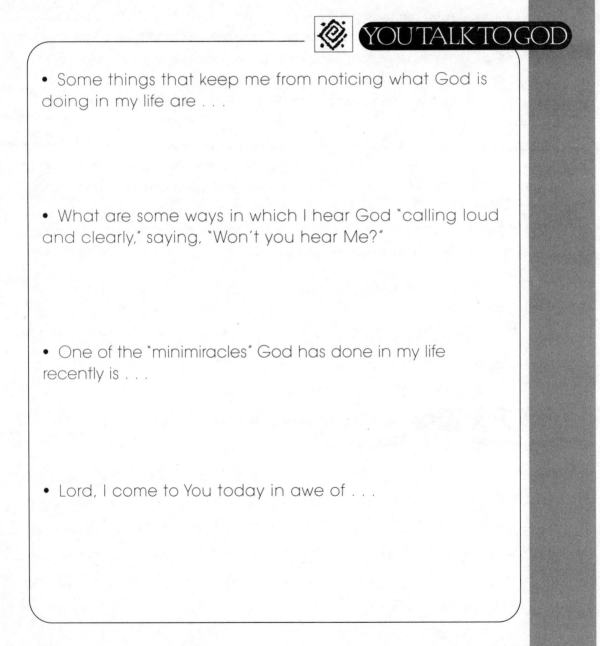

• Some things that keep me from noticing what God is doing in my life are . . .

• What are some ways in which I hear God "calling loud and clearly," saying, "Won't you hear Me?"

• One of the "minimiracles" God has done in my life recently is . . .

• Lord, I come to You today in awe of . . .

29 DON'T GIVE UP

Last year, just after a service at our church had finished, a gentleman came up to me and shared an incredibly humbling, moving story. It was about a young associate of his from work. He told me that this young man's fiancée had left him and, because of the hurt and other things in his life, he was going to give in to the urge to kill himself. The older gentleman then shared how, miraculously, my song "Go and Sin No More" had come on the radio where this young guy was. In a letter, the young man wrote firsthand of his experience:

> I felt a warm hug as I listened. Tears fell like a waterfall from my eyes. (God's) arms hugged me in peace, love, and His amazing grace. . . . I surrendered the war at Jesus' feet. . . . And the peace of God relaxed my mind, body, spirit, and soul. . . . My hunger for God's Word, His passion, and pleasing Him in my life are reminders of His grace toward me. Praise God!

I got to meet this guy in person the other day, which was an incredible experience. That young man's life is such a testimony to God's power. It really proves the fact that God can use anything and anyone to point people to Himself. One of the most powerful things the young man shared with me in his letter was "God is bigger than suicide."

PEOPLE TALK I received a heart-wrenching letter from a 23-year-old single mom in Clarksburg, West Virginia. She wrote,

> Four weeks after my high school graduation I got married. This past January we separated. After 4 months of marriage counseling, we decided to get a divorce. . . . As a Christian, I could not accept the fact that I was getting a divorce. I also hated the thought of dragging our 2-year-old little girl through the pain. I know the devastation firsthand. My parents divorced when I was a year old and I have only seen my dad 5 times in my whole life. I blamed myself for the fact that my daughter would not be able to live in the same house as her father. As shame and isolation engulfed me, I felt separated from God. To escape the feelings of guilt and depression I went back to using drugs and alcohol. But they just piled on more shame, guilt, and isolation.

I began to fill with rage toward everyone and everything. I had been molested and raped by my stepfather when I was 11, and had spent my life trying to erase the memories and ignore the feelings. . . . I just wanted the pain and torment to stop. (It was then) that I planned to take my life. I wrote the letters and had the plan. But my love for my daughter stopped me. Not long after that, I was asked to help drive some kids from a friend's youth group to your concert. . . . (At your concert) I could physically feel God's love and acceptance overwhelm me. I was reminded that no matter what I go through I have the overwhelming power of the living God leading the way. . . . I am learning to relax in His peace and let Him have the battle. ✳

GOD TALKS "We are like clay jars in which this treasure is stored. The real power comes from God and not from us. We often suffer, but we are never crushed. Even when we don't know what to do, we never give up. In times of trouble, God is with us, and when we are knocked down, we get up again." 2 Corinthians 4:7–9 CEV

MORE TIME WITH GOD

2 Chronicles 20:15;   Psalms 37:23–24; 55:22;
Lamentations 3:55–58;   Jonah 2:2–9

YOU TALK TO GOD

• One time when I wanted to give up on something and God gave me strength to carry on was . . .

• If someone I know (including me) ever questions whether life is worth living, I will . . .

• I thank You, Lord, that the battle is not mine, but Yours. Some parts of the battle that I still need to give to You are . . .

Take away my fears. Help me, O God, to trust You.

30 Shootin' Straight

REBECCA TALKS Not too long ago a girl came up to me and said, "Rebecca, I really appreciate you talking about waiting and not having sex before marriage." She explained that when she was 15, she had also made that commitment, but a few years later she broke it. I asked her what happened. She basically answered, "Sin just creeps into your life and takes hold if you're not careful (to stay focused on God)." I then asked what her relationship with her family was like. She responded, "I really believe that if I had been more open and honest with my parents, I probably wouldn't have made the decision I made and I wouldn't have to live with the regrets that I do now." It is so important for relationships in families to be open and honest. And for some that's harder than others because of broken families or non-Christian parents. But, no matter what family we're in, life at home comes with its share of challenges. We've just got to be faithful to live like Jesus no matter where we are or what family we're in.

We all need people who are willing to "shoot straight" with us—people who are not afraid to challenge us in our walk with God. Starting Bible studies or accountability groups is an incredibly cool way to stay focused on God. Invite your friends and family to ask you tough questions like: "How's your walk with God?" None of us can stand alone. When there's honesty in our relationships, there's strength.

PEOPLE TALK The wife of a youth pastor from Lewisburg, Tennessee, wrote:

> After buying your devotional book, God directed me to begin some small group studies of the book. Please be in prayer for us and others as we study. I also keep a prayer book, and I am putting you in it. I will be praying for God to continue to bless your ministry and guide you in your decisions.

Helping one another and praying for one another is so vital to our Christian lives. I need it and so do you.

GOD TALKS "Since God has so generously let us in on what he is doing, we're not about to throw up our hands and walk off the job just because we run into occasional hard times. We refuse to wear masks and play games. We don't maneuver and manipulate behind the scenes. And we don't twist God's Word to suit ourselves. Rather, we keep everything we do and say out in the open." 2 Corinthians 4:1-2 The Message

MORE TIME WITH GOD

 Psalm 15:1–4; Proverbs 16:13; 27:5–6;
Ephesians 4:15

YOU TALK TO GOD

• One of the hardest things anyone ever told me (but I really needed to hear) was . . .

• Someone in my life who "shoots straight" with me is . . .

• Three other people who could become part of an accountability group with me are:

    1.

    2.

    3.

What are you waiting for? Ask them today!

Lord God, help me to be totally honest with You, myself, and others who know and love me.

31 BROKEN BONES

REBECCA TALKS While we're traveling on the road we try to take some time out for intense Bible study. On the "All About God" tour, I remember one study in particular that was led by our bass player, Tracy Ferrie. He shared a whole bunch of Scriptures with us, which was one of the things that made me enjoy the study so much—I love the Bible! One verse especially stood out to me: "Let the bones you have crushed rejoice" (Ps. 51:8 NIV). I shared with the guys afterward what a challenge I thought that was—to rejoice even through painful experiences.

Brad Duncan, one of our two guitarists with shaved heads (who's also a youth pastor), shared a really cool analogy with us. In his own words, this is what he said:

> In that day and time, when sheep were continually straying away, as an extreme measure the shepherd would break a leg of the sheep. Throughout the whole healing process, the shepherd would gently hold the sheep, causing it to become dependent on its shepherd. Once the lamb was healed and capable of running away, there would be such a bond that it would stay closest to the shepherd, having experienced loving restoration.

> What really struck me was how painful it must have been for the shepherd to do that to his sheep even if it was for its own good. It made me realize how God must grieve when He has to allow us to go through pain. But He can really use painful experiences to draw us into an intimate, loving relationship with Him, as we learn to stay close and rely on Him.

PEOPLE TALK I received a dear letter from a girl in Tennessee. She shared:

> On June 5, 1992 I found out that I had cancer. I received weekly chemotherapy along with spinal taps and bone marrow aspirations for two and one-half years. . . . Then, my sister was my donor for a bone marrow transplant in April 1995. Today I am doing well except for very low energy and daily headaches. . . . The Lord has truly been with me each step of the way and I know that I am only here today by His grace. The Lord has brought my family and me into such a close walk with Him through all of this. He has not only been my Healer and Deliverer, but my Best Friend.

MORE TIME WITH GOD

 Job 5:17–18;   Ezekiel 34:11–16;   2 Corinthians 12:7–10; Hebrews 12:5–11;   1 Peter 5:8–11

 YOU TALK TO GOD

• Looking back on my life, I remember a time when God had to "break me" to get my attention . . .

• Some of the spiritual lessons I learned from that experience are . . .

• A part of my life that God is healing now is . . .

Your grace is more than enough for me to get through times of suffering and pain. When I am weak, You are strong. Thank You, Lord!

32 STEPPIN' OUT

A few years ago, I sang at a prison in Georgia. My dad was kind of scared about taking Mum, my baby sister, and me in there. What he knew, but I didn't, was that over half the inmates were imprisoned because of murder. That day, singing praise choruses with those people was such an incredible worship experience, probably one of the more memorable ones of my life.

The men that had become Christians and really given their lives to God were so serious about Him, so in love with Him, so free. It made me realize that these men behind bars were probably more free than so many outside those prison walls who didn't know Jesus. That experience taught me in a big way that God teaches us amazing things when we step out of our comfort zones and trust Him.

In life, I've found God continually has new and unique ways of teaching me to rely on Him, and as a child of His, I am trying to "live by faith." A prayer that challenges us to do this is, "Confront me, God, with things uncomfortable that I may lean on You."

PEOPLE TALK This past year I've really enjoyed reading a book by Francine Rivers called *A Voice in the Wind.* The main character, Hadassah, has been an encouragement to me because of her purity and her strength (you can tell the characters became very real to me in my life!). She was a slave in a Roman family around the time of the fall of Jerusalem, a first-century Christian Jew who got captured by the Romans when they took over David's city.

I love reading her prayers. One of my favorite ones that speaks of our need to step out in faith reads:

> God, why can't I cry out truth from the rooftops? Why don't I have the courage to speak as my father did? I love these people but I haven't the words to reach them. I'm afraid to speak out and say they're wrong and I'm right. Who am I but a slave? How do I explain to them that I am really the one who is free? They are the captives. Lord, what must I do to make them hear?[1]

A guy wrote to me and likened people to bread. And when you think of it:

• We get stale if we just lie around doing nothing.
• We are made to be consumed; that's when we find our purpose.

MORE TIME WITH GOD

 Matthew 8:5–13;   John 14:11–14;   2 Corinthians 4:18;
Hebrews 10:35–39; 11:1–6

YOU TALK TO GOD

• When it comes to letting go and trusting God, where would I place myself on this line?

Walking by faith   Walking by sight

• The top three reasons I have trouble having faith in what I can't see are:

1.

2.

3.

• A circumstance in which God is calling me to step out and put it in His hands is . . .

• Father, I want to please You by my faith. Help me to trust You when I face this situation today:

33 OUR BROTHER'S KEEPER

REBECCA TALKS   Last year I was extremely challenged by some particular verses out of Galatians 6. In response to those verses, I remember going out and sitting in the middle of my backyard and writing my "Life and ministry mission statement." I started out by saying,

> In relation to the verse, "Make a careful exploration of who you are and the work you have been given" (v. 4 The Message), I wrote, I am a girl who loves God very much. He's my best friend, the center of my life, and I want to share Him with everyone who will listen—be that through my music, sharing from the platform, talking one-on-one, or by how I live my life. I feel that quite identifies the responsibility I have to be my brother's keeper and share Jesus with the people around me.
>
> I then went on to talk about other influences that keep me accountable. These thoughts were initiated by the verse, "Don't be impressed with yourself" (v. 4 The Message): To me this means to have major accountability, to keep time spent with God in prayer and in the Bible a huge priority, because then there is no way I can be "impressed with myself."
>
> One of the other verses that really sticks out from Galatians 6 simply says, "Don't be misled" (v. 7 The Message). I believe that if we apply the biblical principle of being our brother's keeper and stick close to those godly people who "keep" us, we will be strengthened to stay on track.

PEOPLE TALK   Just this past spring I received a letter from a guy in Florida. I want to share part of his powerful testimony:

> When I was young, I truly was a spawn of the devil. I rode with gangs and did a lot of stupid things. After a while I hung out with devil worshipers, and they taught me nothing but pain and hatred. . . . I was taught that I had to be somebody, and I did only wrong to accomplish that. . . . I believed I was

only here to put pain and grief in people's lives, and thought that if I killed myself I would solve the problem.

Before I was about to end my life, my cousin was released from the county jail and came to visit me. After a hug or two, he began to preach to me. I was confused. Was this the person whom I once knew? He had changed, something had happened. As he continued, I saw something in him. I knew not what it was, but I felt a need for it. At the end of the conversation, he asked me to give Jesus a chance, just one night of my life. And so I agreed. I will never forget that night, on my knees before God, accepting Him as He accepts me. And for the first time, I felt loved. . . . Four and a half years later, I know that I have the greatest (Father) and I will tell everyone of the forgiving love of my God.

Praise God for the love his cousin showed him. He understood what it means to be his brother's keeper.   ▨▨▨

GOD TALKS "The group of followers all felt the same way about everything. None of them claimed that their possessions were their own, and they shared everything they had with each other. . . . No one went in need of anything. Everyone who owned land or houses would sell them and bring the money to the apostles. Then they would give the money to anyone who needed it." [Acts 4:32, 34–35 CEV]

MORE TIME WITH GOD

Acts 6:1–4; Hebrews 13:1–3;
1 John 4:11–12; 19-20

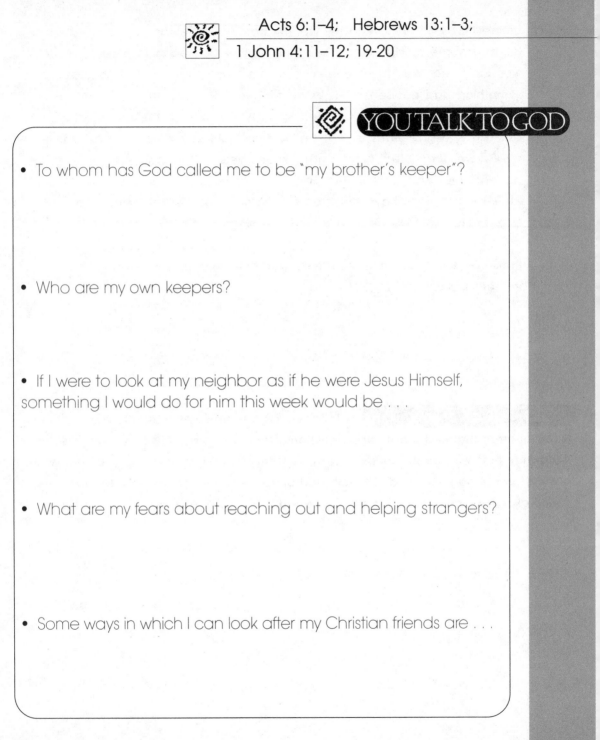

- To whom has God called me to be "my brother's keeper"?

- Who are my own keepers?

- If I were to look at my neighbor as if he were Jesus Himself, something I would do for him this week would be . . .

- What are my fears about reaching out and helping strangers?

- Some ways in which I can look after my Christian friends are . . .

34 TALK ABOUT CHURCH

REBECCA TALKS Last Sunday at church, our pastor reminded us that "if we are in Christ, we are in the ministry." That simple sentence especially spoke to me. I love going to church and getting in the car afterward feeling challenged and encouraged in my walk with God. We have this tradition of going out to eat Chinese food after church. Often, over lunch, we'll talk about the different things we learned through the service. Church fellowship is so important in growing our faith. But, as my pastor said that day, we all have a part to play in the body of Christ. We all have our own "ministry," whether that be within the walls of the church building, or representing Jesus out in the secular marketplace. God calls us to be faithful wherever He puts us.

I remember coming home from youth group sometimes feeling a little discouraged because I didn't think our youth group was growing in God or as serious about Him as I would have hoped. But my dad would always encourage me by reinforcing the fact that God had a plan—that He had put us in that youth group for a purpose. In his own way, Dad would challenge me to be faithful—to be as "serious as a heart attack" about God and to encourage others to be as well. God calls us to be ministers every day, everywhere. And as I learned once, we've got to remember that "God doesn't call the qualified. He qualifies the called."

PEOPLE TALK A teenager from Indiana wrote these words:

> Our generation is tired of the old, run-down stereotypical "dead" church. (We're) searching for something that's going to produce life and give (us) a purpose and a reason to live. That's evident in every form of teenage life if we would just take the time to stop and look at how much (members of our generation) are really reaching out for an answer. . . .

Christianity is not just a "Sunday thing." It's an infinite relationship with the One who saved our soul. Not just once a week, but a 24-7 deal. Twenty-four hours a day, 7 days a week—EVERY WEEK! And until we, as Christians, can truly recognize the importance of having that relationship with the Father, we will never be able to reach out to our generation. We cannot love others until we first lay our petty (differences) aside, sacrifice our lives, and put Jesus Christ foremost. Then, and only then, can we hope to be successful in reaching out.

MORE TIME WITH GOD

 Matthew 16:15–18; Galatians 6:9–10; Ephesians 2:19–22

YOU TALK TO GOD

• What are some of the reasons I go to church? (Check all that apply—and be honest!)

☐ To see my friends.
☐ To ask forgiveness for my sins.
☐ To see a cute guy or girl.
☐ To help other people.
☐ My parents make me.
☐ To worship God.
☐ I want to learn more.
☐ It's something to do.
☐ Other _____

• Which of these are good reasons, and which are bad?

• If I could create a church service that would really meet the needs of my friends, what things would I include?

• The next time I go to church, I plan to do the following in order to encourage someone else . . .

35 CONSEQUENCES

One of the things I love to do in my spare time is to go "hang out" down by the creek on our farm. Often I'll pray or read or skip rocks across the surface of the water. Once when I was throwing small stones in the water and watching the ripple effect, I realized how much that simple action is like our lives. Just like those stones, every decision we make affects so many people around us.

It's a lie that says, "Do whatever you feel like as long as it doesn't hurt anybody." What people don't realize is that every decision we make affects other people in either positive or negative ways.

I enjoyed getting to know two fellow Aussies last year as we toured together. Serene Allison and Pearl Barrett, also known as Considering Lily, recorded the song "Consequences" this past year. The lyrics speak to the fact that there is a ripple effect to all the decisions we make in life.

LYRICS FROM "CONSEQUENCES"

Chorus
You can't do anything, anytime, anywhere without thinking about it.
There's consequences, consequences.

Choices are easily made, sometimes hard to erase,
That's the price we pay for living.
Everything's dark when your eyes are closed,
Left or right, fork in the road,
Play with a bomb and it's going to explode,
Deeds are dominoes.

Repeat Chorus

There's consequences, there's no way around it.

Decisions seem like a bore but they're harder to ignore,
Deciding what you're living for.
Throttle the moment but the moment dies,
Make your own truth but it's all a lie,
Try to speed up and find that life will pass you by.

Up or down, fast or slow,
All I know is that the boomerang will circle 'round
Back to the hand where it was thrown.

Words and music by Brent Milligan and Serene Campbell. © 1997 Up In The Mix Music/River Oaks Music/Alright Bug Music (BMI). (administered by EMI Christian Music Publishing.) All rights reserved. Used by permission.

I received this letter from a 19-year-old guy in Nebraska:

Our generation is like a vacuum: it sees something bad and then gets pulled in toward it. Society portrays all these things as being good and doesn't show the consequences. Why don't we see commercials on television about the harmful things that drugs and alcohol do to the body? . . . Everything we do, watch, or hear influences a person in one way or the other. It is very cool the way God uses people to fulfill His plan. Since God is the potter and we are just the clay, He uses good and bad situations to mold us. Every time we interact with people we make some kind of impact on their lives, whether it is positive or negative.

MORE TIME WITH GOD

 Proverbs 11:17–19;   Proverbs 22:8;   Jeremiah 17:9–10;
Hosea 10: 12–13;   Romans 2:5–11

YOU TALK TO GOD

• A time when I did something good and reaped positive benefits was . . .

• A time when I did something bad and suffered the consequences was . . .

• A decision I made that had a great effect on others was . . .

Help me, Lord, as I seek to follow Your plan for my life. Show me the short-range and long-range consequences of decisions I will make today.

36 LONELINESS

REBECCA TALKS After a concert last year, a young man with a physical disability came up and asked a simple, but profound, question: "What is the cure for loneliness?" My heart just sank for that poor guy, and at the time I really didn't know how to answer him. But, later on, I was thinking about his question and remembered times of loneliness in my own life, especially in my early teen years.

Coming from another country and having to start all over in building new friendships (especially since I was being home-schooled) was really hard for me. I remember coming home from youth group sometimes and crying. I talked to my parents about it, and they reminded me that in order to have friends I would need to be a friend (Prov. 18:24). I needed to get out of my comfort zone, reach out, and not just expect people to reach out to me.

Every day we see so many people who are hurting and lonely and need us to share Jesus' love with them. Can you imagine what would happen if each one of us, as Christians, would take that responsibility to love seriously? Revival would break out!

When we're feeling sorry for ourselves, God calls us to give ourselves away by serving others. And, by doing that, we actually have the privilege of serving Him! We are to pour ourselves out for God and for other people. That's when we find true joy in life.

PEOPLE TALK A girl from Georgia had similar experiences with loneliness. She wrote:

I just moved here from Oregon last year. God has blessed me so much by this move. By being lonely myself, I finally see the people that so desperately need God's love. I've been forced to go beyond my comfort zone, accept failures, and face humiliation, but it's forced me to really depend on God. Through daily devotions, prayer all day long, and a little character molding, I've truly fallen in love with Jesus. I can't even describe the joy I feel. And, for the first time in my life, I enjoy God's truth with unbelievers, doubters, and even struggling Christians. God has made His presence so real to me.

I once read in a girls' magazine, *Brio*, "The best gift we can give to this world is a life lived for Jesus Christ."

GOD TALKS "Each of you has been blessed with one of God's many wonderful gifts to be used in the service of others. So use your gift well. If you have the gift of speaking, preach God's message. If you have the gift of helping others, do it with the strength that God supplies. Everything should be done in a way that will bring honor to God because of Jesus Christ, who is glorious and powerful forever. Amen."

1 Peter 4:10-11 CEV

MORE TIME WITH GOD

 YOU TALK TO GOD

• You withdrew to lonely places to be alone with Your Father. Help me to seek You more in these ways:

• You were a stranger on this earth, as were Your followers. I long to live with You in heaven forever. Prepare me for that heavenly home in the following ways:

• Help me to look for others more lonely than myself. I may see them at:

> • School . . .
>
> • Home . . .
>
> • In my neighborhood . . .
>
> • At work . . .

• Those whom You are calling me to minister to are:

• I will show Jesus' love to them in the following ways this week . . .

• The next time I feel lonely, here's what I'll do :

Lord, when I am confronted with times of loneliness, help me to look to You and learn from Your example.

37 FASTING

REBECCA TALKS Last year, after a 3-month tour, I got to go back to Australia for 2 weeks. Really my whole purpose for going back was simply to have some "time out" with God. I had been feeling pretty exhausted, and I really believe God allowed me that time away just to rest before Him.

So, I spent a week away with my grandma, to pray, to read my Bible, and to fast. It was the first time I'd felt strongly challenged to fast, and it was such a refreshing experience. This is what I wrote in my diary before the trip:

REBECCA'S JOURNAL

God just confirmed that I am to fast for a period of time while in Australia. I got out Mum's *Life Application Bible* and was about to look up fasting in the concordance. My eyes were drawn to the bottom of the page that says, "Fasting—going without food in order to spend time in prayer—is noble and difficult. It gives us time to pray, teaches self-discipline, reminds us that we can live with a lot less and helps us appreciate God's gifts."

I looked up the word *fasting* in the concordance—God is hitting me over the head with this (Thank You, *Lord*)—and found that we fast to "inquire of the LORD," to "seek help from the Lord" (2 Chron. 20:3–4), to "humble ourselves before our God" (Ezra 8:21 NIV), to petition Him (Ezra 8:23). Pretty cool stuff—the Bible rocks! 🙂🙂🙂

PEOPLE TALK According to the *Life Application Bible,* a fast was "a period of time when no food was eaten and people approached God with humility, sorrow for sin, and urgent prayer. . . . In the Old Testament, people often would fast during times of calamity in order to focus their attention on God and to demonstrate their change of heart."

GOD TALKS "When you practice some appetite-denying discipline to better concentrate on God, don't make a production out of it. It might turn you into a small-time celebrity but it won't make you a saint. If you 'go into training' inwardly, act normal outwardly. Shampoo and comb your hair, brush your teeth, wash your face. God doesn't require attention-getting devices. He won't overlook what you are doing; he'll reward you well." Matthew 6:16–18 The Message

MORE TIME WITH GOD

 Nehemiah 9:1–3; Isaiah 58:3–12;
Joel 2:12–15

YOU TALK TO GOD

- In the Bible, people fasted for at least 5 different reasons:

    1. Confession of sins (1 Sam. 7:5-6)
    2. Mourning (2 Sam. 1:11-12)
    3. Petition for specific needs (Ezra 8:21-23)
    4. Preparation (Matt. 4:1-2)
    5. Commissioning (Acts 14:23)

- An unconfessed sin in my life is . . .

- Something for which I am sorry is . . .

- Something I am seeking God for is . . .

- Something God is preparing me for is . . .

- A ministry for which I need to fast is . . .

38 ARE THEY CURIOUS?

REBECCA TALKS I love Christian T-shirts. In fact, about every time I see someone at an airport wearing a Christian tee, I go up to them and say, "Cool shirt!" even if I don't know them from Adam. But, you know, regardless of what we wear on the outside, God cares infinitely more about the state of our hearts. The question to us is, Christian shirt or not, Do people know by our actions and lifestyles that we're Christians? Can people see a love, a joy, and a sense of purpose and hope that can come only from knowing Jesus? Can people see a difference in us? More important, what does God see when He looks at our hearts? I hope that He finds deeply imprinted the words, "God rules here!"

PEOPLE TALK A friend of mine in Cincinnati, Ohio, told me the following story:

> I was returning from a trip to California when one of the flight attendants stopped and asked, "I'm just real curious. What does John 3:17 say?" She probably had heard of John 3:16 before, but not of the verse that follows it. She had seen that verse written on the back of the baseball cap I was wearing. I went on to explain the verse to her, "For God did not send his Son into the world to condemn the world, but to save the world through him" (NIV). The front of the cap says, "Save Planet Earth." You never know when what you're wearing will give you an opportunity to share about Jesus' love.

I was excited when I read this report from a girl in Arizona:

> For the past 7 weeks on Sunday evenings, our church has been going through a course on witnessing to our unsaved friends. It has been so awesome to learn how to really tell people about Jesus! I will be praying for boldness in our generation, so that we can reach the many unsaved kids our age.

GOD TALKS "Honor Christ and let him be the Lord of your life. Always be ready to give an answer when someone asks you about your hope. Give a kind and respectful answer and keep your conscience clear. This way you will make people ashamed for saying bad things about your good conduct as a follower of Christ." | 1 Peter 3:15–16 CEV

MORE TIME WITH GOD

 Acts 8:34–35;   Philippians 2:14–16;

Colossians 4:4–6

• When it comes to sharing my faith in Jesus with others, where would I place myself on the line below?

bold witness   silent witness   no witness at all

• My biggest fears concerning talking about Jesus are . . .

• Three people in my life who desperately need a relationship with Jesus are . . .

1.

2.

3.

• A way in which I can help each of them is . . .

1.

2.

3.

• Help me, Lord, to live out the gospel in my life this week by . . .

39 SMELL THE ROSES

Check out this story I wrote in my diary a while ago:

REBECCA'S JOURNAL

Just now I found Libby, my 4-year-old sister, quietly sitting at my desk and I got worried. She never does that. I started to drill her as to what she was doing (what mischief she was getting into, really) and she said, "Just sitting quietly . . . watching the sun . . . trees . . ." I told her I like to do that too. She asked, "Why?" And I said, "Because they (the trees) blow in the wind." She said, "Cool . . . I love it."

My little sister had it figured out. In life, we need to stop and smell the roses, appreciate the moment, count our blessings, and ultimately praise God for it all!

PEOPLE TALK   I remember a commercial in Australia for Kellogg's Corn Flakes. It said, "It's the simple things in life that are often the best."

"He (man) cannot be content unless he praises You (God) because You made us for Yourself and our hearts find no peace until they rest in You." —St. Augustine, in his *Confessions*   ᎶᎶᎶ

GOD TALKS

"Open your mouth and taste, open your eyes and see—how good GOD is.
　　Blessed are you who run to him.
　　Worship GOD if you want the best;
　　worship opens doors to all his goodness." Psalm 34:8-9 The Message

MORE TIME WITH GOD

 Psalms 100:1–5; 147:7–11; Proverbs 10:6;
Isaiah 64:3–4

 YOU TALK TO GOD

- I come to You, Lord, thanking You with all of my senses;

  - A taste I thank You for is . . .

  - A smell I praise You for is . . .

  - One of Your blessings I see but sometimes take for granted is . . .

  - Something I hear and thank You for is . . .

  - Something I feel and give You praise for is . . .

- I pause right now to count all of the blessings You've brought into my life:

40 A "JESUS PERSPECTIVE"

REBECCA TALKS   Of all the women in the world (and I'm sure there are many others that I just don't know about yet), I believe Mother Teresa has one of the strongest "Jesus perspectives." Here's a quote of hers that I wrote in my diary once:

> Jesus said, "What you did to the least of my brethren, you did to me." Therefore, the only sadness I ever feel is if I do something wrong, if I hurt our Lord in some way, through selfishness or uncharitableness, for instance. When we hurt the poor, and we hurt each other, we're hurting God. Everything is His to give and to take away, so share what you've been given, and that includes yourself. Jesus, in all His New Testament words, always had such a selfless heart, a "God's-will-not-my own" attitude. I so desire to have that continually.

I came across a really cool Scripture in Chronicles that I paraphrased like this: "And you (my daughter), acknowledge the God of your father, and serve him with whole-hearted devotion and with a willing mind, for the Lord searches every heart and understands every motive behind the thoughts. If you seek him, he will be found by you" (1 Chron. 28:9 NIV).

PEOPLE TALK   A 15-year-old girl from New York asked,

How do you know God is talking to you? How do you distinguish God's voice from your own? I'm asking because I think God is beginning to show me how He's gonna use me. But, I really want to be sure, 100 percent positive that it's God, and not my own ideas.

She concluded her letter by sharing these lyrics with me, a poem she had put to music:

A Servant's Prayer

Lord of my life, I bow before You,
Lord of my life, how I adore You.
You created the wind, You created the sea,
But yet You still love me.
Help me, O Lord, to see Your way,
Help me, O Lord, to give You all my days.

Reveal Your face in all I see,
Help me become all I can be.
I love You, dear Father, with all my might,
And I'm thankful You'll be here all of my life.

Used by permission.

I believe this poem/prayer is evidence that God is speaking and using her to encourage others to center their perspectives on Jesus.

A youth pastor shared with me this nugget of wisdom: "God has to remain in the center of who we are and what we do and why we exist."

GOD TALKS

"Solomon, my son, worship God and obey him with all your heart and mind, just as I have done. He knows all your thoughts and your reasons for doing things, and so if you turn to him, he will hear your prayers. But if you ignore him, he will reject you forever." 1 Chronicles 28:9 CEV

MORE TIME WITH GOD

 Psalm 25:4–10; Psalm 143:8–10;
Hebrews 8:10–11; 1 John 5:14–15

 YOU TALK TO GOD

• Lord, I ask You today to teach me to do Your will in the following areas:

• Show me where I should go . . .

• Show me what I should do . . .

• Show me Your perspective as I face this situation today . . .

Other devotional materials Rebecca recommends as followup after reading *You're the Voice* are:

- *Time with God*. NCV Word Publishing. Daily Full Year Devotional/Bible.
- *Experiencing God Bible Study*: *Knowing & Doing the Will of God*. Henry T. Blackaby and Claude V. King,
- Bibles: **The Message**—NAV Press; NIV;**The Promise Bible for Students**— Thomas Nelson.

11

1.   Francine Rivers, A Voice in the Wind, (Wheaton, Ill.: Tyndale House, 1993),234.

20

1.   Tim Hansel, You Gotta Keep Dancin', (Colorado Springs, Colo.: Chariot Victor Publishing, 1986), 55. Used by permission of Chariot Victor Publishing.

24

1.   Rivers, A Voice in the Wind,

27

1.   For more information, or the opportunity to sponsor a child through Compassion International, please call: 1-800-336-7535.

ABOUT THE AUTHOR
LIFE ON THE ROAD

When I was approached to share my thoughts and impressions of life on the road with Rebecca St. James, I was both excited and relieved. Excited, not at the thought of seeing my words in print, but excited to be able to open the door of the tour bus and take you, the reader, into the realm of life on the road with RSJ. The relief I felt came from knowing that people like you will gain an insight into what goes on behind the scenes with Rebecca and the team. In times where the private lives of some of our most respected ministers seem to explode in a contrary existence to the one portrayed from the pulpit or stage, I was relieved to be given the opportunity of not only speaking firsthand from an outsider's point of view about Rebecca's life, but of encouraging people like yourself to strive to live out a God-centered life—such as the one she anchors herself to.

Rebecca is the first person to say she's just a normal, everyday 19 year-old. She has the same likes and dislikes, ups and downs, that any average teenager has. The difference, however, is the fact that her relationship with Christ and her desire to please Him, worship Him, and live for Him, rather than for all the things around her—color and influence everything she does. In reality, this shouldn't be unusual for a Christian. This should be the norm by which we all live.

In Corinthians, Paul speaks of conscience. That piece of us tells us right from wrong. We all have this conscience, we all have the ability and the knowledge of knowing not only what is right and wrong—but also what pleased God and, conversely, what angers Him. In my time with Rebecca on the road, I couldn't help but feel that God was nothing but pleased with her. Not because she preaches the gospel and has a powerful ministry, but pleased in her as a child, a daughter of His, simply living her life in accordance with Him and a heart that is hungry to know Him more and more.

In many ways, what the audience sees onstage is such a small amount—a "snippet" of all that makes up Rebecca. Sure, she can sing, write songs, entertain, and preach up a storm—but if you were to ask her what is important to her, I'm sure that none of these things would be mentioned. Don't get me wrong, she loves serving the Lord and His church through what she does, but it is obvious that her relationship with God and her family are the top priorities for her. You see, her service, her ministry, is not her whole life. She has the firm understanding that it is not what you do that is important, but who you are.

So, you want to know who she is? Well, it would be presumptuous of me to assume I know all about her. All I can do is act as a witness of what I saw in the time I was with her and her team during the "All About God" tour. What I saw in my time so encouraged me that my hope is to encourage you in the same way.

You see, living your life according to God really isn't difficult. Sure, it takes a bit of discipline to begin with, but God gives us the strength and wisdom to continue living for Him.

From reading all of this, you may start to get the impression that the whole crew lives the life of constant prayer—in silent reflection and meditation, somewhat akin to nuns in a convent; or perhaps they walk around with a supremely serene expression on their face like Mother Teresa. This, however, is totally unrealistic and I can assure you not the way things are for Rebecca. Like I said earlier, she's just your average 19 year-old. She doesn't float along 3 inches above the ground surrounded by a soft haze of pastel tones. Rather, she listens to Third Day, Jars of Clay, and loves running around the family farm with her five brothers and little sister, Libby.

Likewise, life on the road is kept to as much of a "normal" family life as is possible. Therefore, the entire family (except for the chickens, the dog, and rabbit), travel together in one of the two RVs that make up the convoy. Somewhat like the Partridge family (except the bus isn't yellow), everybody has a role to play. Many people wonder about schooling, so yes, the kids are home-schooled—but not only learning the 3 R's in the bus—they then find themselves working in an environment usually reserved for adults. Whether it be technical, behind the scenes, backstage, or out front—the education continues.

One of the great things about this team is the sense of community and their way of making outsiders (like me) feel part of the family. Family is a strong, all-encompassing aspect of Rebecca's ministry. No one is treated any differently and there is a strong understanding of each person pulling his or her weight, all working together to serve for the common good in the ministry. The impression I received was that Rebecca is more or less the public face on a ministry that involves many more people behind the scenes. No one person is more important than another—one body, many parts. An example of this would be in one of Rebecca's jobs, which is to clean the tour vans each day. Sweeping, dusting, tidying, and cleaning the bathroom. Would you believe she actually enjoys this?

The days on tour are almost always long. Can you imagine getting up and going to school/college/work at 7 A.M. and not getting to sleep until 2 A.M. every day? The days include long drives, physical work in the setup and pack down, but also (thankfully) plenty of laughs. It is as though the sense of humor and "no-secrets" policy of each person, along with the grace of God, keep the machine well oiled. Of course, there are times when tensions arise, but because of the openness and the sense of free speech, these are settled quickly before resentment is allowed to take hold.

I realize that for many people, life on the road may seem glamorous or perhaps even like an extended summer camp. Maybe you're even reading this and expecting to hear such things. This, I believe, is a myth that is fueled by the mainstream music industry. In this context (generally speaking) their lives are controlled not only by parties, drinking, and sex, but by perpetuating the sense of mystery about their lives. For them, part of the appeal lies in being "famous." Whereas for the Christian artist, truly dedicated to serving the Lord, his or her life should really be an example that everyone can follow—realistically. In this way, Rebecca realizes that she is just a normal person and, in every respect, lives a normal life. She goes to work like most of us—albeit a rather unusual job—and serves her Lord the best way she knows how.

Perhaps I have disappointed some of you who were hoping to hear all the juicy tidbits of inside info—but actually, the great part is that there is nothing to tell! I could tell you about the funny songs that come from the band's bus, the steady diet of fast food, the never-ending stream of chicken dinners or a certain keyboard player's fascination with visiting every Wal-Mart in North America, but let's face it . . . all that stuff is trivial. The real meat in the matter is lives lived in service to God. That is the reality, that anyone, no matter what your circumstance or background, can achieve. The fact that you're reading this very book, *You're the Voice: 40 More Days with God*, is testimony that this is the desire of your heart. Through this book you'll hopefully discover more of Rebecca's heart—reading her thoughts and her own journal entries. My prayer is that you'll discover the simple fact that we are all equal in God's eyes—regardless of whether we sing and minister to thousands or faithfully work at a fast-food restaurant. What we do is irrelevant—God sees the heart.

God bless,
CR